A
PATHÉTIQUE SONATA
FOR THE
CAGED CHILDREN

悲愴奏鳴曲

A PATHÉTIQUE SONATA FOR THE CAGED CHILDREN

A
PATHÉTIQUE SONATA
FOR THE
CAGED CHILDREN

悲愴奏鳴曲

APPASSIONATA FUGUE MELODIES
INK-BRUSHED UNDER CALLIGRAPHIC ART

WING-CHI CHAN

NEW ACADEMIA PUBLISHING SCARITH
Washington, DC

New Academia Publishing, 2020

Printed in the United States of America

Library of Congress Control Number: 2019916010
ISBN 978-1-7330408-6-0 paperback (alk. paper)

SCARITH An imprint of New Academia Publishing

NEW ACADEMIA PUBLISHING

New Academia Publishing, 4401-A Connecticut Ave. NW, #236,
Washington, DC 20008
info@newacademia.com - www.newacademia.com

Contents

Introduction:
The Magic and The Magician

Wing-Chi Chan is a classically trained musician and an expert in its western canon; and so, we might believe he'd write with meter and rhyme. In this book he jumps off from his traditional education to design a new style in literature. Tonal writing depends on a compression and expansion of line lengths and a repetition of sounds. He uses aesthetics on the page and word count to attack large social issues. Injustice cannot be presented lyrically ***('Sonata for Caged Children'***) and he redefines beauty to serve his purposes. Breaking old forms to create new ones is an awareness that Wing-Chi Chan intends as influence.

Wing-Chi Chan does not depend upon logic nor does he abandon it – he seeks a more demanding dialect to create emphasis and power on the page. The word choice is always surprising; and for those readers who are used to reading a square verse on a page, well they're in for an awakening.

What's the reward for taking chances in art? Perhaps to make visible an imaginative cultural experience. Wing-Chi Chan's poems are monologues, hymns, chants and prayers. He asks a lot of the reader and of himself. He asks that we understand that formal constructions cannot house meta-concepts. He is, in turn, concrete and abstract, playful and serious.

A usual reaction is to question nonconformity and perhaps to resist the unknown; but as one reads this work, perceptions change into an anecdotal dreamworld. Wing-Chi Chan writes of ruptures within our society and during our time. His social criticism manifests itself into a rigorous new form with its own set of rules. His psychological horizon also finds beauty in the world, and much to honor and praise; he shapes and forms his tiny operas and then terms them "tonal poetry." The tone represents a place for change; the poetry is conceptual art. **A ONE TIME ONLY MASTERWORK OF ITS KIND** never to be repeated or imitated. Making something never seen before is magic and Wing-Chi Chan is the magician.

Grace Cavalieri, Maryland Poet Laureate

Praise:
A Unique Poetic Landscape

Wing-Chi Chan's poetry marks a unique departure from all conventions. Yet it also embodies all the intricacies of form and genre across linguistic boundaries. His poems are written in English but conceived in both English and Chinese. As a bilingual poet, his subjects and sensibilities are deeply human and universal.

Trained in music and ethnomusicology, Wing-Chi has a special predilection for sound and tonal structures: symphonies, sonatas, fugues, cantatas, themes and developments, variations of all kinds, motifs and recapitulations, harmonies and counterpoints, pizzicatos and pianissimos, songs and their emotive transformations (e.g. *None But An Appassionata Serenata*) etc., etc. He then transfers such sonic metrics and textures into a unique poetic landscape with carefully coordinated metric "shapes" and rhythmic patterns. Each line, therefore, contains a hidden sound of music that is yet to be written. We can even read his poetry as hidden music scores.

Those who know classical Chinese poetry can appreciate even more his inventiveness in transposing its rhyming conventions into their counterparts in English. Wing-Chi takes great liberties with the usage of the English language precisely because he is familiar with the rigid rules and conventions in classical Chinese poetry that has been developed over centuries. In breaking them down he is able to reinvent a linguistic universe of his own. I hear vague echoes of composers Edgar Varèse and Chou Wen-chung.

However, for Wing-Chi Chan, art is never created for its own sake, since he harbors a deep-seated compassion for the sufferings of humanity everywhere. ***A Pathétique Sonata for the Caged Children*** is an illustrious case in point. Here, on a vast poetic canvas, one feels the pathos of a committed humanist who cares deeply for all the victims of tyranny and massacre. History resounds between his poetic lines as he tries to remind us of the endless cruelties that mankind has inflicted on themselves. Few poets today are capable of aspiring to such lofty heights as this self-styled global citizen.

Leo Ou-fan Lee, Ph.D.
Professor Emeritus of Chinese Literature, Harvard University
Chair Professor of Humanities, The Chinese University of Hong Kong

An Echo:
Some Observations on
A Pathétique Sonata for the Caged Children

Wing-Chi Chan's second poetry anthology consists of stanzas embedded with classical music in voice, going hand in hand with the art form and aesthetics of traditional Chinese poetry and calligraphy. As a historian, I am impressed of Wing-chi's poetic imagery and metaphors for vividly portraying a wide range of modern world's humanity issues. And I am delighted to echo my observations on that period of history.

"Scientia potentia est" is a Latin aphorism meaning "Knowledge is Power", the origin of which is attributed to Sir Francis Bacon, scientist, educator, Lord-Chancellor, and an early giant in the Age of Reason in 18th-century Europe. It was believed that knowledge based on reason through education would enrich humanity, and the spread of education through shared knowledge would improve human potentials and achievement. Wars and atrocities, believed to arise out of ignorance and misunderstandings, would be greatly reduced if not totally eliminated. The universality of mankind was close by man's fingertips only if education spreads, so as the Enlightenment thinkers believed. Thus, the government has taken over the task of educating the youth as one of its important functions since modern times.

For almost a century, the call for reason and logic, together with the slogan for equality, fraternity, and freedom of expression, played havoc in the face of political revolution leading to social unrest and war in the developing countries. Generations of youth all over the globe have sacrificed their lives to achieve these values. Thus, the acquisition of knowledge through education seems no panacea to continuous war and suffering.

Whereas the ideals of the Enlightenment thinkers led the way in the May 4th student demonstrations in 1919, and a continued struggle for an open and fair society ushered in the Beijing Massacre on June 4th in Tiananmen Square seventy years later; the Imperial Army of the Emperor Hirohito killed and raped Chinese civilians when they invaded Nanking in 1937, motivated by a nationalistic drive spoon-fed by the Imperial State.

It is equally dangerous when power falls into the hands of ambitious politicians, even in Western democracies. The tragedies of Kent State and Jackson State Universities could perhaps have been avoided if reason and mutual understanding had prevailed.

The killings narrated in ***A Pathétique Sonata for the Caged Children*** were all tragic events of a massive scale that would have dumbfounded the Enlightenment thinkers. Neither knowledge nor education can eliminate war. Wisdom through humanity is perhaps more preferable than knowledge through education. Knowledge can be a gateway to many killings without contributing to the moral issue of right and wrong in the human dimension.

Chan, a trained musician and bilingual poet, is uniquely qualified for this task. Even from reading through the lines, one can visualize the suppression of the youth combatting against the authorities and hear their anger, shoutings of despair, and jubilation of victory, the tinkling of the Samurai swords in the Nanking suburb and the rolling of tanks and cracking machine guns at Tiananmen Square. As part of the audience, I come out with a melancholic feeling about this continuous human tragedy in our times. Indeed, the success of this masterpiece owes to the multimedia training and sensitivity of its talented composer and author, Wing-Chi Chan.

Steven K. Luk, Ph.D.
Former Director for The Chinese University of Hong Kong Press
Faculty for General Studies, Hang Seng University, Hong Kong

FOREWORD

The prolific Wing-Chi Chan is back with his second book of poems. As with his first, Wing-Chi flies high and far as each line is like a belt around the world. He recognizes no disparate connections between words — they join to penetrate our consciousness so that our intuition sees his subjects from the inside out. Even the geometric shape of his poems has meaning. You'll want to read Wing-chi viscerally. Just leave your reason out of it. He's not talking to that part of you.

—A. B. Spellman, Poet & Witness to Jazz
Former Deputy Chairman, U.S. National Endowment for the Arts

As with any new artistic creation, one may initially be puzzled by Wing-Chi Chan's innovative style during its first encounter. Further immersion into his work, however, leads to fresh experiences about the world around us. Drawing upon principles of Chinese philosophy and arts as well as Western concepts of musical form, Wing-Chi has forged a new type of poetry that serves as a **"commentary of current affairs"** on topics of social injustice, war, and other human experiences. By utilizing the theory of sonic metrics, individual lines are reordered to create versions of varying tension, texture, density, and rhyming rhythm. Each line of the poem invokes specific images that touch upon the deepest of our emotions, yet the entire poem is cast within a clearly defined structure and rhyming scheme with sonic and visual influences. These poems reconnect us to history, to the real world, and to our personal lives of hope and loss, love and pain, and conflict and reconciliation.

—Eric Lai, Professor of Music Theory
Baylor University, Texas

Overall, ***A Pathétique Sonata for the Caged Children*** is an ambitious, highly engaging, dynamic work – full of interesting plays in complexities and cares. The scope of this collection is wide. It comes in three sections: History and Poetry;

Life and Poetry; Culture and Poetry. The effect is rich, highly varied, far reaching, political, international, historical, contemporary, universal, personal – by turns light and tender and sad and joyful – and an arresting blending of Chinese and American.

—Michael Whelan, Irish American Poet/Retired Writer for The World Bank Board Governor, Arts Club of Washington

In Wing-Chi Chan's newest poetry collection, he takes up the human condition in both language and music to shape unique pieces that open the heart. His work is a chorus of voices from many perspectives, ages, and genders. Each poem rings with truth and empathy and each poem commands its own sound of meaning. This cultural overlay of thought, word and music mastered here make way for a new sight and understanding of the poetic spirit that embraces the entire globe and all of humanity. Wing-Chi taps into his great ability to bring forth that, which resides in the depths of the human heart. This requires a new path and Wing-Chi has courageously set the course.

—Sheila Carter-Jones, Ph.D.
Author of Three Birds Deep/Former Professor of Education,
Chatham University

Reading this manuscript of words and emotion flung across the page, I can't help but imagine an exhausted conductor at the end of a symphony, ravished and ravaged by his work. Wing-Chi Chan has created a work that should be sung to be appreciated even as we read the pain and outrage caused by humanity—that is, while this work borrows from music and art for its expression, it begs to be performed. And I hope that it will be performed, this libretto of rage. And I hope that when that happens, the world listens.

—Joanna Howard, Professor of English, Montgomery College/Coordinator, A Splendid Wake, Poetry Archival Program at George Washington University

The poems in this collection, like the poet, at least to this reader, can be infuriating. Often, I found myself asking why did you use that word? Did you really mean to say that, or is that a typo? What alliterative audacity! Likewise, these poems can be invigorating like the rat tat tat beat of a drum behind a Sonny Rollins solo. But always they are eviscerating as they slash through conventional forms, puncture idiomatic expressions, and cut deep into the heart of social injustice.

I have known Wing Chi-Chan for over thirty years as a musician, composer, conductor, writer, translator, impresario, and champion of justice. We first met at St. Elizabeth's Hospital for the Mentally Ill in Washington, DC. Not as patients, but as counselor and translator for a newly arrived immigrant patient. Not content to merely serve as translator, Chan helped find an exit strategy from the hospital for this poor man and then cleared a path for his successful transition to our society. Over the succeeding years Chan has continued to challenge and impress me with his imaginative associations of the arts (visual and aural), history, and social justice. Many a night I would receive a call from Chan seeking help for some poor individual who had been trampled under the heel of blind justice. Many a day I would receive an email from Chan highlighting a particular passage of music, poetry, or visual art.

This collection of poems is not for the faint hearted. They do not feint with dewy spring morns and crumpet crumbs across the breakfast table. Rather they have the wide, heavy stance of an aging boxer, ready to knock you down the minute you drop your guard. Having been so clubbed after reading this collection, I did eventually get back up off the mat, and while the music was still ringing in my ears, picked up the collection a second time and heard for the first time the musicality inherent in these poems. The fight was over. It was brutal, but worth it.

—*Curt Hansen. Attorney at Law, VA/DC/MD*

Wing-Chi Chan's Poetic Landscape: Calligraphic Art Vitalized

Under Integrated Rhythmic Brushes & Sonic Metrics

1. **Rhythmic Brushes**

Touches under Guqin-zither Art

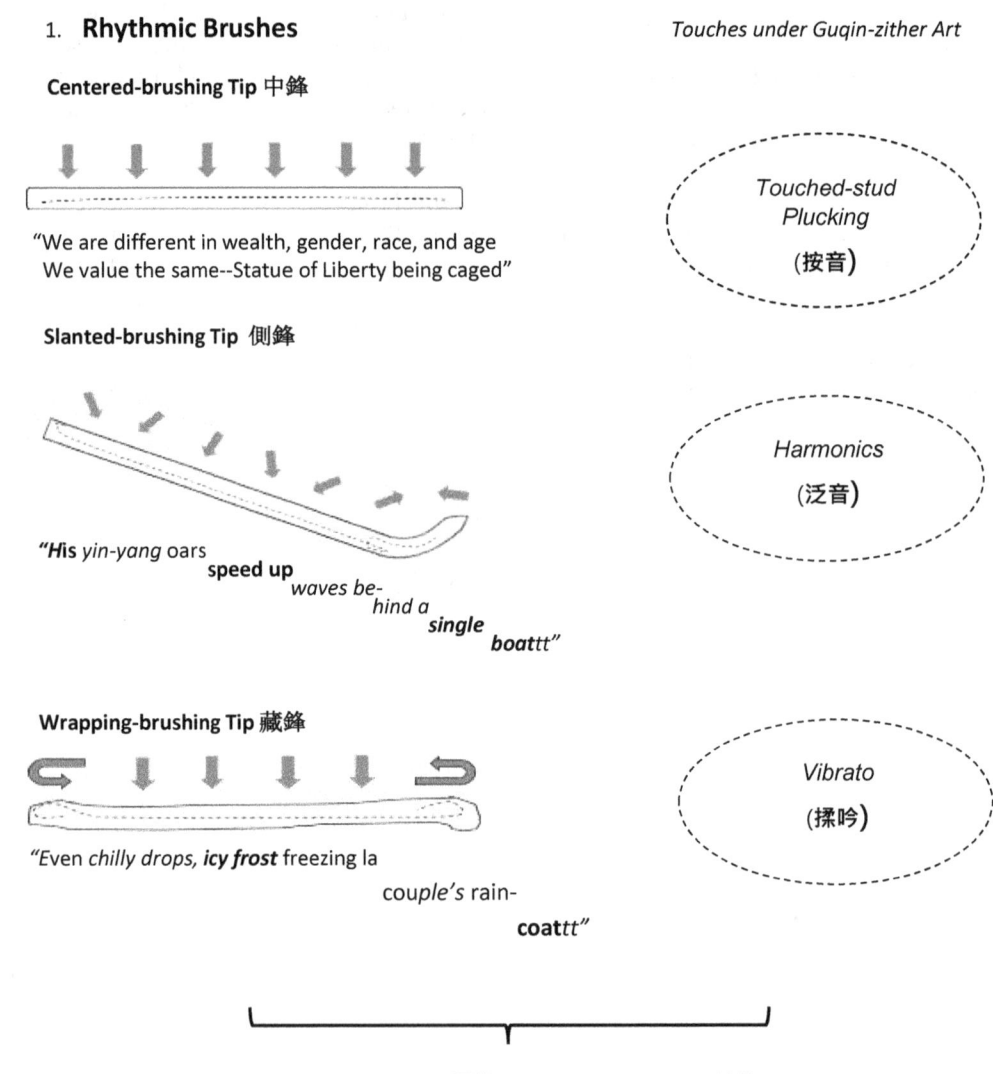

Centered-brushing Tip 中鋒

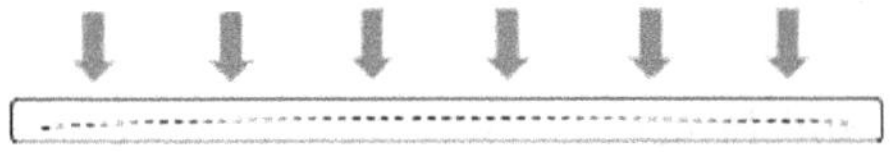

"We are different in wealth, gender, race, and age
We value the same--Statue of Liberty being caged"

Touched-stud Plucking

(按音)

Slanted-brushing Tip 側鋒

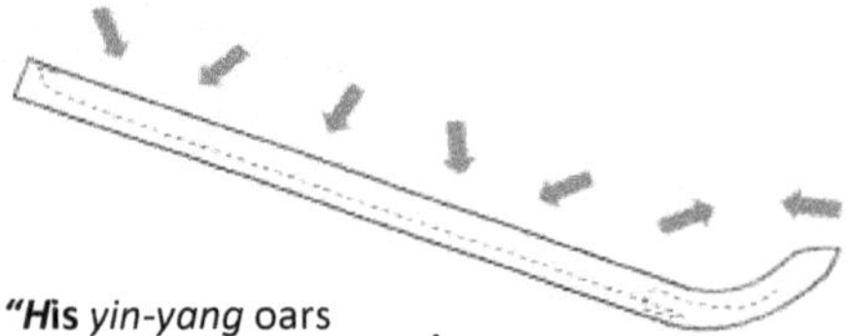

"His *yin-yang* oars
speed up
waves be-
hind a
single
***boat**tt"*

Harmonics

(泛音)

Wrapping-brushing Tip 藏鋒

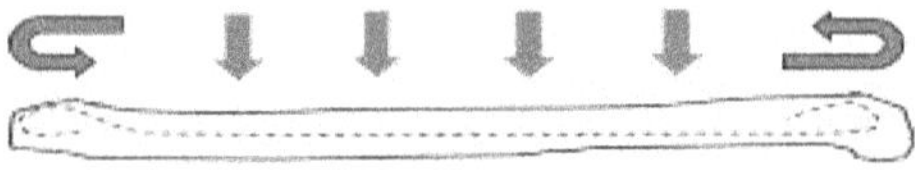

"Even chilly drops, ***icy frost*** freezing la
coup*le's* rain-
coat*tt"*

Vibrato

(揉吟)

Returning - brushing Tip 回鋒   Twist - brushing Tip 轉鋒

2. Sonic Metrics

Aesthetics of Wing Chi's Poetry

Yin – Yang
Positive – Negative
Spatiality

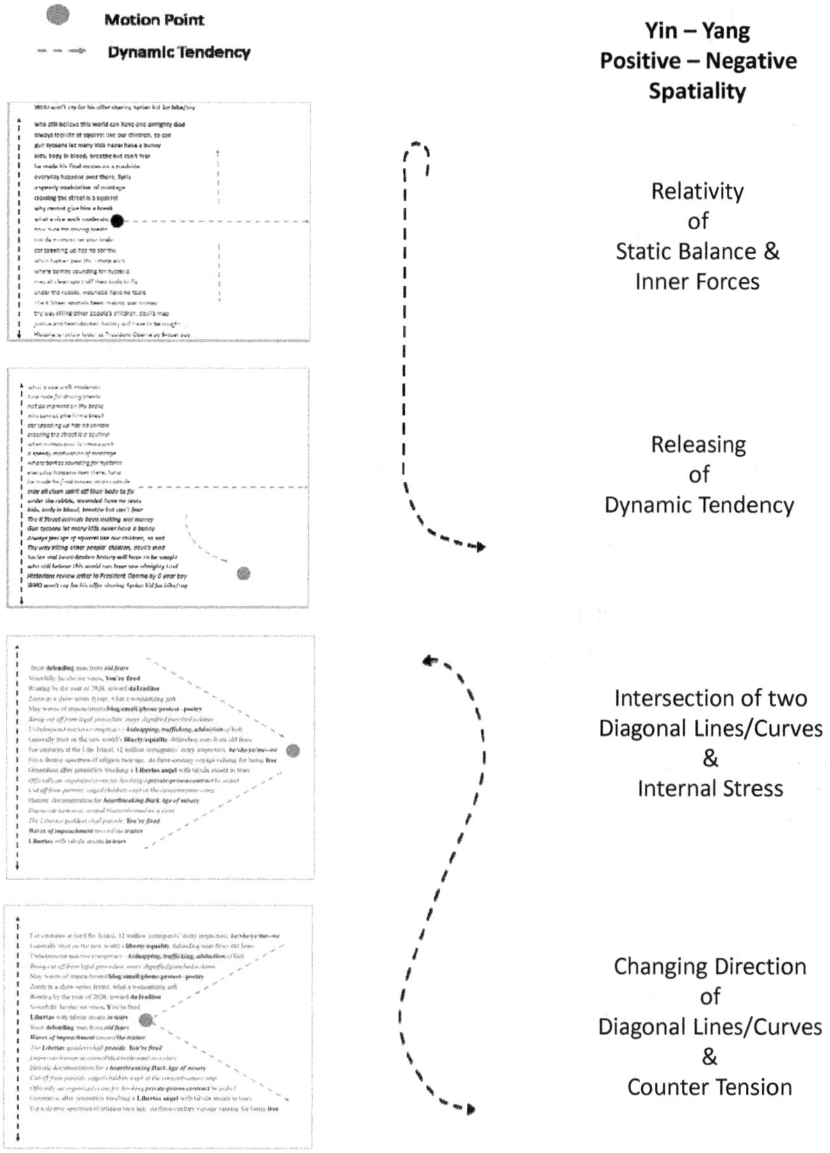

3. Brush-work & Ink-work Vitalized Via Integrated Poetic Textures/Spatiality

There has been a connective link between traditional Chinese calligraphy and poetry whereas Chinese calligraphy transcends the content of a poetic landscape onto an aesthetic form in terms of 3D modeling, rhythmic movement and power of strokes. These aesthetic elements could be presented by its layout arrangements, as well as treatment for brushwork and inkwork. Wing Chi Chan's application of calligraphic art in utilizing computer fonts is monumentally inventive. There are basically five operating principles to execute various kinds of stroke which are correlated to each other for forming an integral structure and rhythm, mainly for the following brushing tips.

1. *Centered-brushing Tip* (Zhong Feng 中鋒) No matter under which direction of motion for the brush to move, the Centered-tip will always be brushed within the middle space for a stroke. Providing the brush to be held perpendicular to the writing surface, the "sharpness" of the tip enables the hair of the brush-pen to spread out evenly that subsequently the strokes will be fully enriched of strength and vigor.

2. *Slanted-brushing Tip* (Zè Feng 側鋒) In contrast to the Centered-tip, Slanted-tip is used for brushing bend, fold, square and/or angular strokes.

3. *Wrapping-brushing Tip* (Cáng Feng 藏鋒) Wrapping-tip enables the "sharpness" of the brush hairs to be hidden within the moving strokes between the beginning and final touches of the brush tip on the paper. Then the characters impart an intrinsic power for not mentally revealing the total strength under the hand motion of the calligrapher. That the sustaining energy implicitly demonstrates an invisible reservation of philosophical vitality.

4. *Returning-brushing Tip* (Huí Feng 回鋒) Returning-tip means turning the brush tip just a little bit for the purpose to splash an opposite direction of stroke different from the original motif. The sharpness of the brush tip will then be touched a little bit circularly within the same stroke.

5. *Twist-brushing Tip* (Zhuǎn Feng 轉鋒) is used to develop a round dot brush moving continuously in a circular motion.

In integrating with the aesthetics and skills of Chinese calligraphic practice, Wing Chi has been foremostly breaking through the conventional boundary of his original Chinese language's rhythmic brushes and sonic metrics, and creating a new dimension of touches under Guqin-zither art for his English poetry. Yet Chan may even be recognized for the 3D impact that he has been merging, inheriting and innovating for a totally new cross-cultural art form on texture and spatially for wordscape. What a beyond-one-single-language-poetry peak!

Lai-Fong Wong, Ph.D.

Poet/Artist/Faculty for Educational Psychology, The Chinese University of Hong Kong
Art Curator, The Airport Authority Hong Kong

PREFACE

APPASSIONATA FUGUE MELODIES INK-BRUSHED UNDER CALLIGRAPHIC ART

On ***May 4, 1970***, a team of seventy seven Ohio National Guards, fully armed with M1 Garand rifles, inexcusably shot at a group of hundreds of unarmed students at a parking lot during the students' anti-war rally, protesting against the bombing of Cambodia by the United States military forces, inside the campus of the Kent State University in Ohio. That ***May 4 Massacre*** resulted in the death of four students and nine wounded. Again, ten days later on ***May 14***, police shot two unarmed African American students to death and wounded twelve at ***Jackson State University***, a historically black college in Jackson of Mississippi. These events led four million students to protest nationwide, subsequently shutting down four hundred fifty high school and college campuses. Their collective voices had a ripple effect—Four years later, President Richard Nixon was forced to resign from his office on August 9, 1974, amid bipartisan impeachment on the ***Watergate scandal***. Similarly another historical moment on May 4 of 1919, tens of thousands of Chinese college students in Peking (Its current Romanized name is Beijing) and later in other cities, ignited the beginnings of an intellectual movement, known as the ***May-Fourth Movement***, to protest against the Western powers' volatile manipulation of the ***Versailles Treaty at the Paris Peace Conference***. The historic signing notably outlined the settlement and concessions of *World War One.* Although the Republic of China was considered to be one of the winning countries at time, this treaty forced China to cede its sovereignty of Shandong Province, which has been famed as Confucius's home province, to Japan. However, during the war, the Nationalist Chinese Government sent over 140,000 non-combatant laborers to the front battlefields in Europe that caused 20,000 deaths. After experiencing such an international humiliation, the student movement mobilized to form a roaring new generation of nationalistic Chinese literati, and to import two core values of Western civilization: ***Democracy and Science***.

As a global citizen, I have been fortunate to teach at the Capital Normal University in Beijing, lecture at Yale/George Washington/American/Columbia Universities, and commit to poetry activities in Washington, while maintaining daily contact with colleagues, friends and students around the world.

On one side, as a literati/poet/musician/commentator, I shoulder a Confucian mission to remonstrate, in a form of crystallized epic, on any unfair and unjust social issues (興觀群怨 Xing/Guan/Qun/Yuan, Metaphor/Commentary/ Communication/Expression). On the other side, I am privileged to live in a civil society that has been safeguarded by the stipulated ***constitutional rights on the freedom of speech and of the press.*** It is this minimum level of freedom that inspires me to cultivate my instinct for social commentary on the current affairs, without fear of retaliation or political persecution. Moreover, it has been a personal epoch to use online technology in searching for information and knowledge from the mass culture and cross-academic disciplines, free from authoritarian censorship.

Subsequently I am able to employ various illustrative fonts to vitalize a modern visual ***wordscape*** which displays the vocal technique of ***vibrato tremolo,*** and a textured ***density of calligraphic art for point, line, shape, curve and spatiality,*** encapsulating a vision of the twenty-first-century ***pointillism, stratification, minimalism and serialism,*** in ***mirroring*** of the ***ink-brushing fugue melodies*** on an unsung passion derived from ***a pathétique sonata for the vulnerable***.

Inside my ***pathétique wordscape***, I attempt to construct a poetic imagery built upon a ***synchronized rhetoric/sonic/visual architecture*** envisioning on the **aesthetics** of ***brevity, abstract and allusiveness,*** which is centered on an extended art form of ***fugue sonata*** in a metaphysical perception, i.e. by the intrinsic scheme of A B A' (Exposition Statement—Tension Derived from Variation/Development of Themes—Recapitulation for Relaxation). It cores on the ***niche of a contrapuntal condensation of pathos and ethos rhetoric*** that is, ***being mounted between melancholic and Zen mood***, as well as ***toned between satirical and empowering timbre***, crafted on the foundation of ***a passionate yin-yang chemistry.***

Being enlightened by an enriched spectrum of multi cultures, I am wholeheartedly ***indebted to*** **Ludwig van Beethoven**'s revolutionary sonority which was rooted in his heroic compassion and tender heart that embraced both pride and sorrow; to Chinese-American composer **Chou Wen-chung's** (1923-2019) musical philosophy of the calligraphic art and of the single-tone entity, and to French-American composer **Edgard Varèse's** (1883-1965) aesthetics on sound-mass integration and on the endless pulse of serialization; so as to Iraqi-British lady architect **Dame Zaha Hadid** (1950-2016), "Queen of the Curve", whose design on the flowing curves thoroughly demonstrated the art of a continuo variation on her chosen theme that could be considered as being in fugue with the fluid dynamics.

Also I sincerely **dedicate this poetry anthology to** all caged civilian and literati victims who have been vulnerable to violence/massacre under tyranny and war crime, including the thousands of ***undocumented children*** who have been involuntarily removed from their parents by force and ***caged along the border today***, and the thousands of unforgettable students and civilians ***who lost their lives*** to tanks and machine-guns ***at the Tiananmen Square on June 4, 1989***.

Last but not the least, I hereby ***salute to those gladius literati*** around the globe, who strive for ***fundamental freedoms*** to express their own speech and opinions in confrontation with tyranny and censorship.

An Unsung Aria For The Ineradicable White Terror

Casablanca ***ag***ents turned their hometown in **b*lood***
Blowing off a First Aid ***girl's eye*** in a meter by distance
Days **later,** *beating* every passenger *at metro--**Fuck***up
Teargassing **chemica*l* wea*p*ons** *at underground sta*tion
Waves of **terrorism *crime*** *under* forensic documentation
***Weeping page*, it *began a dark* age**
Journalist's *eye shot--Laws for* what
Frame-up ***suicide***/Killings for ***genocide***
Citywide Victoria Gong/So brave & strong
Thugs with **no identification *claimed as cops***
Storming academia's **Eden Garden** ***like mobs***
Beasts ***stomped*** on **heads** of teenaged *boys*
Bloody **tor*ture***--How could ***but*chers** enjoy
*Students assaulted/***raped,** tourists ***humi*liated**
Doctors **handcuffed** *& thousands* **perse*cuted***
10,000+ **tear*gas* canisters** been sh*ot*
Arr*est* of **the pregnant/*elite*--***on* same *p*lot
Soil/air under ***di*oxin** *contamination*
Toxin of **sperm cell *for generations***
Shoo*ting*, *bea*ting, kick*ing*, *la*ughing, yel*ling*, *scre*aming, *cry*ing, recording, fi*l*ming
The **world** has been ***watch*ing**
***Night*mares *re*call**
Pains/suf*fering *all
B*e*a*u*ti*f*ul *l*ives *lost*
Ty*ranny* **ugly** *sm*all
*Brea***king** *iron* wall
Voice of civil *f*orce
Hal*lelujah* to Lord

育我劬勞維港城　一城歌泣自由聲　少男少女斑斑血　寧不視頻魂魄傾

ACKNOWLEDGEMENTS

At the 50th anniversary of the May 4/May 14 shootings at Kent/Jackson State Universities in 1970 & the 101st anniversary of the May 4 Movement in China in 1919...

To my grandparents, parents, elder sister, relatives/teachers/friends, who are now smiling in heaven, had experienced unspeakable human pain and humiliation caused by political/socio-economic war and the after effects of colonialization of the 20th through 21st century;

To all of my siblings, family, colleagues of the Federal Poets, and students who, by sharing of their individual experiences, knowledge, expertise, and feelings, have unquestionably enriched the spectrum of my cultural understanding and artistic insight;

To mentors/colleagues Grace Cavalieri, Leo Ou-fan Lee, A.B. Spellman, Steven K. Luk, Eric Lai, Michael Whelan, Sheila Carter-Jones, Joanna Howard, Curt Hansen, US Congresswoman Grace Meng, Maryland Senator Susan Lee, former New York Senator Marty Golden, Kang-I Sun Chang, Tang Muhai, Han Kuo-huang, Jan Bach, Tim Blickhan, Donald Funes, Harrison Ryker, Ho Hsiu-hwang, William Wan Hon-cheung, Edith Wu, Lee Pak-ho, Sandra Beasley, Char Jones, Katie Wong, Thomas Bensen, Liu Kwok-fai, Anna Lawton of the New Academia Publishing, and the many unsung heroes who have helped make this book available to the public; to late Professors Chou Wen-chung, Jao Tsung-I, Kishibe Shigeo, Cheung Sai-bung, Paul Steg, Lee Chiu-yuan and Shelly Davis;

To Wong Lai-fong for her cover design/graphic illustration, John Wang and Koon-Sea Hui for their calligraphy works, and Eddie Kang for his photography;

To William Chin for his support of the publication, & Michelle/Michael Chung for their proofreading;

To millions of intellectuals who were forced to flee away on foot, 1937-45, from Kweilin and Peking;
To heroic World-War-II Flying Tigers who saved millions of lives over a temporary capital Chungking;
To da gladius girls & boys who have sacrificed flesh and blood just for letting their civil liberties sing;

Chansons Dedicated to the Unsung Victims/Heroes

<山河熱血濃>---調寄沁園春
曉月盧溝, 刁斗沙風, 漏夜急衝。 薊北刀光颯, 兜頭劈殺, 鬼神驚煞, 土赤泥紅。
八一三魂, 四行倉庫, 旗正飄飄敵愾同。 金陵恨, 懦夫遺弱女, 倭獸逞凶。
江山半壁城空, 浩氣燕歌, 夷狄動容。 嗣台兒莊捷, 穿湘入蜀, 流亡千里, 扶老携童。
瀝膽長沙, 仁安羌役, 還我山河熱血濃。盟軍識, 芷江英雄劍, 銘鑄青龍。

<魂兮恁筆鳴>
風吼紫荊花折聲　少年兒女楚歌傾　蒙塵草木殤悲切　捨我魂兮恁筆鳴

I am most humbly indebted.
Wing Chi Chan June 4, 2020 陳詠智

My passionate messages in Chinese

<惜緣適伊>

彈鋏天池　辯晰華夷　屈子騷絲　莎氏諷辭　挽轡朝思　夕譜觴詞　瞠目弗詩　落霞訴遲
一路蓑衣　九曲三癡　瀝膽擒魑　魂息失依　惜緣適伊　滄泊微時　跋履渠知　氣凝兩儀

<漢家陵闕誰識> 一 調寄念奴嬌

摘瀟湘月, 抹星斗, 霜露簷前嬌滴。問子規啼, 腔節激, 琴劍知音冷覓。
大浪淘沙, 平沙落雁, 滾拂揉呤剔。刑場弦剔, 廣陵千載堪憶。
堪砭毛火株連, 逼人倫滅絶, 榱崩渠憶。幾代儒林, 經史黜, 渠辯華夷今昔。
悉索胡言, 依權謀竄匿, 忝談朱色。韶風塵竭, 漢家陵闕誰識。

<凝浩氣招魂> 一 調寄滿江紅

鐵膽金戈, 銅琴戚, 崩雲霹靂。存凜烈, 百年英烈, 捨生折戟。
拳亂屈降圖革命, 命懸鏖戰情堪憶。平津陷, 沿火海淞江, 燕歌澀。
金陵劫, 荊鼓激, 湘桂撤, 殤讎積。甫擎杯祝捷, 自殘相逼。
幾輩沉淪渠貶斥, 一朝得位誰珍惜。劍膽魂, 凝浩氣招魂, 淩空擊。

註: 拳亂乃八國聯軍之役

<擲筆問二君>

其一　蔣門何故疊光頭　介入江湖落濁流　石表難填千古恨　黃鐘毀棄鑄冤仇
其二　髦朝一世斲源頭　拆國無情陷劫讎　東主御批周宰輔　帝愁青史董狐修

<誰為共和冤斷頭>

百年辛亥史家憂　誰為共和冤斷頭　士失恒心君失道　府無綱紀院無謀
官欺庶子如芻芥　眾視衙差若寇讎　革命何期流熱血　依然血淚染神州

<橫過萬重山>

平生橫過萬重山　際合陰晴轉眼翻　碧澗流泉飄九曲　幽蘭碣石憶瑤環

<甘甜爽夾香>

涼瓜火腩炒生薑　開胃甘甜爽夾香　醉饗蒸炆煲仔菜　久違滋味焗魚腸

<肝膽陳辭> 一 調寄風入松

離鄉負笈未離詩, 浪跡問新知。取經飲馬京畿路, 遊於藝, 傾吐憂思。
望道天人際合, 醉情譜曲填詞。
勾弦弔伐國殤時, 亮劍不遲疑。騷魂翰墨他鄉賦, 擂鼓動, 肝膽陳辭。
海角子規拂斥, 禮崩樂壞何依。

<唐韻入英詩> 一 調寄浪淘沙

泊岸度新詞, 船笛茲茲。鬢毛疏落電車時, 堪訴百年家國事, 何訴嫌遲。
唐韻入英詩, 韻律癡癡。聲詩彼岸遇相知, 拈字腔圓丁板外, 拈刮於思。

註: 垂十年始就以格律賦英詩之詩集 Mass For Nanking's 1937

<一舟横得月> — 調寄臨江仙

汨水西潮籲鼓辟, 抛腔問字聲圓。放歌蹄沓逐山穿, 竹林琴跡絕, 無乃士蒙冤。
韻砭東流天地隙, 恁憑霜骨封存。惜緣投止九重淵, 一舟横得月, 長嘯扣雲端。

<罹七十年劫> — 調寄水調歌頭

罹七十年劫, 容嘆夕陽紅。 起初光復心切, 毛蔣渝相逢。
秋夕高堂把盞, 春至沙場喋血, 三歲易彝鐘。草莽湊丁板, 韶夢恨成空。
天下得, 綱常失, 罡劫重。分崩離析, 魂兮肝膽瀝江東。
絶世梟雄癲煞, 幾代封侯剩刮, 衙內窟蒼龍。還拗春秋筆, 通鑑古今同。

<物我空靈>

一劍傾情　兩文入聲　三語韻馨　四象分明　五行軸承　六合修平　七夕孤星　八音濁清
九脈歸鈴　十方協鳴　百代含英　千載流形　萬嘯西荆　億兆篇盈　無我神凝　物我空靈

<耶魯士相逢>

欽賢尊長閫家風　次考方圓御六龍　康復罡風羈煞劫　宜家耶魯士相逢
註: 張欽次大哥習工程,耶魯大學孫康宜教授尊翁曾罹十載羈劫,撰冠首韻,恭申敬忱!

<五四書生夢>

書生五四上街頭　白話文風濟九州　德賽匡時猶是夢　百年沉劫罔天讎

<笑傲江湖> — 和東坡琴詩

琴猶在匣已聞聲　聞劫不平刀鞘鳴　絶響臨刑聲煞上　廣陵焉是指間聽

<誰説不值錢>

誰説豪情不值錢　横風逆雨踩沙田　沉橋轉馬飆星月　一馬平川撼九天

<哀弔泣貞辭> — 調寄浪淘沙

魂斷下關時, 叫喚妻兒。 金陵一夜遍横屍, 弱女凄聲遺國恥, 殤祭遲遲。
哀弔泣貞辭, 逐筆心撕。 七旬誰輓斷腸詩, 弦壓九州鼙鼓逼, 瀝血依依。

<鑑史激懷>

馬上挪九鼎　兵強未強國本　餓莩如山反資反舊　蹂躪深層道德　誰識其極惡
牀緣禍全民　黨固非固綱常　冤案遍地無法無天　殤殘數代家庭　史誅此窮兇

<望道天涯海角魂>

涉重洋闖異方　披星追臘月　霹靂飆白塵　去留肝膽雨瀟瀟
固予彈鋏横戈　袖捲莽莽天涯網
沿淺澗依星斗　踏雪採寒梅　雰霜淼銀鬢　登落嶽巖風淡淡
何妨撫弦望道　襟懸氳氳海角魂

HISTORY

&

POETRY

3

A PATHÉTIQUE RHAPSODY ON LOCKDOWN

Life
Dark
Virus
Brea*thing*
Epidemic
Ca***tastro***_phic_
Disea*se Muta*tion
Glo***baliza***tion
Various **ages**
Masked ***fa***ces
Smog_gy_ s***ky***
Lock*down*

Solo
Plato
Legato
Staccato
Immortal
O sole mio
Torna Surriento
Pizzicato
Piccolo
Mortal
Misso
Bravo
Taco
Hun**gry/**De***pressed*** *War*
Pain**s/*suffering* all**
Beautiful lives **lost**
Night***mares*** *recal*__led__
Brea***king*** **so**cial ***wall***
Voi_ces_ **of** glo***bal*** for**ce**
S_ing Halle_***lujah*** *to* **Lor**d

Light
*Dea*__th__
Stro_king_
Pande**mic**
CO*VID* **19** Vi***rus***
Ur*banized* pol**lu**_tion_
*Cros*__sed__ *in*__fec__*tion*
*Be*ing en**caged**
*Be*yond *ra*__ces—*Clean*__ air *fi*__ne__
Gre***en t***own

Rhapsody is hereby referred to a potpourri of popular melodies, with an epic or heroic character, for free fantasies.

A PATHÉTIQUE SONATA FOR THE CAGED CHILDREN

For centuries at the Ellis Island, 12 million immigrants' entry inspection, ***he/she/ye/me--we***
Generally trust on the new world's **liberty/equality** defending man from old fears
*Unbeknownst massive conspiracy—**kidnapping, trafficking, abduction** of kids*
Being cut off from legal procedure, every dignified punches da damn
May waves of impeachment/**blog/email/phone/protest--poetry**
Zoom in a show-series tyrant, what a womanizing jerk
Roaring by the year of 2020, toward **daTraditor**
Voicefully he/she/we voice**,** **Y**ou're fired
Libertas with tabula ansata ***in tears***
Trust **defending** man from ***old fears***
Waves of impeachment** toward **the traitor
*The **Libertas** goddess shall **preside**, **You're fired***
Deprecate human as animal that enthroned on a shirt
Historic documentation for a ***heartbreaking Dark Age of Misery***
Cut off from parents, caged children wept at the concentration camp
*Officially an organized crime for hooking **private-prison contract** be unbid*
Generation after generation touching a **Libertas angel** with tabula ansata in tears
For a diverse spectrum of religion/race/age, da three-century voyage valuing for being **free**

Trust **defending** man from ***old fears***

Voicefully he/she/we voice**, You're fired**

Roaring by the year of 2020, toward **daTraditor**

Zoom in a show-series tyrant, what a womanizing jerk

May waves of impeachment**/blog/email/phone/protest-poetry**

Being cut off from legal procedure, every dignified punches da damn

*Unbeknownst massive conspiracy—**kidnapping, trafficking, abduction** of kids*

Generally trust on the new world's **liberty/equality** defending man from old fears

For centuries at the Ellis Island, 12 million immigrants' entry inspection, ***he/she/ye/me--we***

For a diverse spectrum of religion/race/age, da three-century voyage valuing for being **free**

Generation after generation touching a **Libertas angel** with tabula ansata in tears

*Officially an organized crime for hooking a **private-prison contract** be unbid*

Cut off from parents, caged children wept at the concentration camp

Historic documentation for ***heartbreaking Dark Age of Misery***

Deprecate human as animal that enthroned on a shirt

*The Libertas goddess shall preside, **You're fired***

Waves of impeachment** toward the **traitor

Libertas with tabula ansata ***in tears***

For centuries at the Ellis Island, 12 million immigrants' entry inspection, ***he/she/ye/me--we***

For a diverse spectrum of religion/race/age, a three-century voyage valuing for being **free**

Generation after generation touching thy Libertas angel with tabula ansata in tears

Generally trust on la new world's liberty/equality in defending man from old fears

*Unbeknownst to massive conspiracy—**kidnapping, trafficking, abduction** of kids*

Officially an organized crime for hooking la **private-prison contract** *be unbid*

Cut off from parents, caged children wept at such concentration camp

Being off from legal procedure, every dignified punches damn, damn

May waves of our impeachment: blog/email/phone/protest--poetry

Historic documentation for a heartbreaking Dark Age of Misery

*Zoom in a show-series tyrant, **what da womanizing jerk, jerk***

*Deprecate human as animal **that enthroned on shirt, shirt***

The Libertas goddess shall preside & rule—***You're fired***

Roaring by the year of 2020, **towards one Traditor**

Waves of impeachment to a dictator's new shirt

Waves of voiceful voices**, "**You're fired, jerk"

Trust for **defending** man from thy ***old fears***

Liberty Statue with tabula ansata ***in tears***

Private-prison contract--crime, *unbid*

***Massive kidnapping/abduction** of kids*

Voices for centuries, he/she/ye/we

Valuing for a spectrum being **free**

Toward **da traitor**, you're **fired**

Note: **Ellis Island**, north of Liberty Island, in Jersey City of New Jersey, had served as the gateway for each of the 12 million new immigrants' entry inspection upon his/her arrival to the United States from 1892 to 1954.

The **Statue of Liberty**, on Liberty Island in New York Harbor, has been an icon of freedom welcoming new immigrants entering from any foreign countries whereas a Libertas goddess holds a torch above her head on her right hand. Meanwhile in her left hand, the goddess carries a tablet *tabula ansata,* inscribed in Roman numerals, of July 4, 1776, that is the date of the United States of America's Declaration of Independence.

On the popular United States television program series ***Apprentice***, during the years of 2004-2016, many emerging contestants would be roughly removed by the host Donald Trump, with a trade-mark-typed closing, "**You're fired**!"

From the 12th to 16th of June, 2019

I Exposition

On June 12, unknown cops mad, mad

Shooting press/spraying mom-What's a suck

Thou unarmed peacefully sang *Hallelujah to the Lord*

Pearl of the Orient splashes a landmark stoned on vitality

Symphonizing diverse spectrum of strata from a civiliance/brilliance

LAM claimed herself good mom/ignored students cleaning aftermath with no token

Crossing over East and West, fishing port became a financial hub in the name of Hong Kong

Seeded from kids' tears, sweat and blood, this city from now on makes us be da civic strong

Who could label kids making riots--A night nobody made single piece of glass broken

Dated on 16th, civil voices roaring in mountains of over two millions

Global media captured live evidence of da police activity

A girl crossed her legs, sat in front of cops' shield wall

Beating boys/girls, whose batons full of blood

Recalling theirs, every mom still sad

II Development

June 12, **cops *mad***
ddddddddddd

Recalling theirs*ssssssssssssssssss*, **mom**
Sad
adadadadadadad

Beating....batons.....b*lood*
odododod
Shooting press/spraying mom...a s***uck***
A **girl......***in front of cops*' **shi*eld wall***
Sang*ggggggggg*
peacefully
***Hallelujah* to the Lord**
.......media captured......activity
P*earl of the* Orient
a landmark stoned on vi*tality*
on 16th....v*oices....*of
over
two *millions*
*Sym*phonizing**.........a**
civi*liance/bril*liance
............k*ids***.........ri***ots*---**A ni*ght*** *nobody made single piece of glass* **broken**

claimed...good mom/ignored *students* **cleaning** *la aftermath with no* **token**

Crossing **over** East and *West*
*.....a financial hub.....***Hong Kong**
from kids' *tears, sweat and blood*,
this city
.......*be*
***da* civic strong**

III Recapitulation

On June 12 unknown **cops mad/*mad***

Recalling theirs, every **mom** *still* ***sad***

Beating boys/girls, whose **batons** full of ***blood***

***Shooting press/spraying mom*-What's a suck**

A **girl** *crossed her legs*, **sat** in front of ***cops' shield wall***

Thou **unarmed *peacefully*** *sang* ***Hallelujah to the Lord***

Global media captured live evidence of da **police activity**

Pearl of the Orient *splashes a landmark* ***stoned on vitality***

Dated on **16th,** civil ***voices roaring*** in mountains of over **two millions**

Symphonizing diverse ***spectrum of*** strata from la ***civiliance & brilliance***

Who could l***abel*** kids making **riots--**A night ***nobody made single*** *piece of* **glass broken**

LAM claimed herself good mom/ignored students ***cleaning da aftermath*** *with* **no token**

Crossing over East and West, fishing port became a ***financial hub*** *in the name of* **Hong Kong**

Seeded from **kids'** tears, sweat and **blood**, this city from now on makes us be *da* ***civic strong***

Note: The United Kingdom used modern warships to invade and defeat Manchurian China during the **First Opium War** in 1842. As a result, Hong Kong Island was ceded to Britain. With an area of only 426 square miles, Hong Kong has been praised for its magnificent harbor, otherwise known as the ***Pearl of the Orient***. In 1997, Hong Kong was returned to Socialist China under the 1984 Sino-British Joint Declaration for maintaining Hong Kong Special Administrative Region's free economy structure that is to be safeguarded by a judicial system of common laws for a period of fifty years, so-called ***One country, Two systems***. Today Hong Kong has become the second most densely populated region with a population of 7.5 million of various nationalities; the Hong Kong Stock Exchange has been ranked as the third-largest one in the world. However the 2019 Extradition Bill, which was initiated by its Chief Executive (That position is equal to a Governor) Carry Lam, has been erupting of continuous citywide protests and social turmoil for months. Lam, who was NOT elected under universal suffrage, described the police operation on June 12 as a matter for educating the naughty kids at a press conference on the 13th. In response, over two million peaceful civilians marched to protest for their civil liberties on June 16; the protestors did not leave a single piece of broken glass on the street. In fact, numerous school teenagers voluntarily cleaned up street by street the next morning. Subsequently I compose my weeping Chinese poems as follows.

<吻你重光見>一調寄菩薩蠻

當街淫暴綱常褻, 千家啜泣肝腸切。徒嘆鬼神殤, 犬徒囂煞張。
逃生時碰面, 吻你重光見。蒙二噁英塵, 一城留血痕。

<恨雕弓挽>一調寄青玉案

茶餐港式香醇啜, 平靚正, 工夫絕。識百年華洋秘訣, 一聲滄海, 幾聲胡越, 幾代人和悅。
煞從仲夏魈魁奪, 摧煞黃花碧濤血, 血染硝煙霻影月, 恨雕弓挽, 射天狼決, 橫塑承天闕。

<家繫獅子山>

千錘萬嚙劫人寰　不忍鄉人血脈殘　翹楚囚兮嗚一嘯　一心家繫獅子山

<刻楹自由時>

隨街火滾鬼吟詩　除夕燒衣化悼辭　申屋嶺凝兒女血　刻楹光照自由時

<怒火沸孤城>

滿腔怒火沸孤城　港九街頭泣隕星　瓜熟黃台摧折摘　太平山蕩不平鳴

<月滿汨殤辭>

今秋月滿汨殤辭　誰忍稚童頻折肢　吟我燕歌神鬼嘯　難嚥餅食點燈時

<討伐瀛秦劫>

攞腔度曲恨無兵　討伐瀛秦怒髮傾　不忿冤魂冤不息　擎天擊筑意難平

<酹酒朝天擊>

夏夢方酣閃霹雷　入秋花折撼瀛錘　橫戈酹酒朝天擊　欲哭鐘鳴一箭催

<噁英催淚中>

傘陣排山剁煞衝　留書訣別遍孩童　紫荊兒女硝烟劫　陰毒噁英催淚中

<恨失自由聲>

天崩鬼泣鳥難鳴　罡煞烏啼月冷清　羈我楚魂秦火獗　圍城恨失自由聲

A LAMENTED CHORUS FOR THE STATUE OF LIBERTY

SUNG AFTER NOVEMBER 8, 2016

We are different in wealth, gender, race, and age
We value the same--Statue of Liberty being caged
We can't believe our civilization could be encaged
We won't let history be ruined on one single page
We're casting the valuable above the dollar wage
We shan't surrender our beings to one bingo sage

What happened last night, a stage of the enstaged
How could democracy system betray many waged

Why *MEN ARE CREATED EQUAL* be raped by a sage
Where civilian teared for our liberty been encaged
When history for a rebirth one day being up-paged
Who rebirths the Statue of Liberty from a Dark Age

Note: November 8 was the United States Election Day in 2016

A SIX-YEAR-OLD BOY'S AIR TO NOBEL PEACE LAUREATE BARACK OBAMA*

** I felt sad after seeing an injured Syrian boy's photo at the ambulance. Then I read a six-year-old American boy Alex's letter to President Barack H. Obama, Nobel Peace Laureate, offering to share his bike and toys with that Syrian boy. Suddenly I witnessed a street squirrel being killed by a cold-blooded driver. Everything happened at once, and my stream of consciousness flooded out....*

WHO won't cry for his offer sharing Syrian kid for bike/toy
who still believe this world can have one almighty God
always feel life of squirrel like our children, so sad
gun tycoons let many kids never have a bunny
kids, body in blood, breathe but can't fear
he made his final moves on a roadside
everyday happens over there, Syria
a speedy modulation of montage
crossing the street is a squirrel
why cannot give him a break
what a nice walk moderato
how rude for driving presto
not da moment on your brake
car speeding up has no sorrow
when human past the timing arch
where bombs sounding for hysteria
may all clean spirit off their body to fly
under the rubble, wounded have no tears
The K Street animals been making war money
thy way killing other people's children, devil's mad
justice and heart-broken history will have to be sought
Historians review letter to President Obama by 6-year boy

what a nice walk moderato
how rude for driving presto
not da moment on thy brake
why cannot give him a break
car speeding up has no sorrow
crossing the street is a squirrel
when human past la timing arch
a speedy modulation of montage
where bombs sounding for hysteria
everyday happens over there, Syria
he made his final moves on a roadside
may all clean spirit off their body to fly
under the rubble, wounded have no tears
kids, body in blood, breathe but can't fear
The K Street animals been making war money
Gun tycoons let many kids never have a bunny
Always feel life of squirrel like our children, so sad
Thy way killing other people' children, devil's mad
Justice and heart-broken history will have to be sought
who still believe this world can have one almighty God
Historians review letter to President Obama by 6-year boy
WHO won't cry for his offer sharing Syrian kid for bike/toy

Note: North-West K Street of the District of Columbia had been marked as the major hub for think tanks and **international lobbying industry** during the period of 1980 to 2012. ***Air,*** originally a musical term for the 17-18th century solo song with a modest and melodic character in Europe, is hereby symbolized as a tiny voice from the common civilian.

FORTY-SEVEN ALEPPO KIDS' ELEGY AT CHRISTMAS

Jesus is two thousand sixteen year as being told
Shamed to have heard from such a ten year old
47 Aleppo kids only ask for something to eat/drink
Nobel Peace Laureate President--What you think
Christians are joyfully singing a Christmas rejoice
Please hear this Syrian boy's fear for his last voice
A video of rubble shows blood of uncivilized cold
An era on missile of ethnic cleansing to be folded
Who tone-death 47 orphans who'd voiced lovely
Who in da name of God force them cryless—Ugly

Who care kids' parents died of airstrike, shelling
Who, the powerless, hark even the angel yelling
Alas, White House's been busy as a farewell base
The boy said tomorrow you could miss their face
Da day we sing Xmas carols that's free to rejoice
Please recall the orphans' fear of a last-day voice
Syrian, tearless, now have nothing to eat & drink
***Gloria in excelsis Deo*, a hymn the kids also think**
I have no hesitation in giving up my personal life
For God's sake **IF** my death will **save the 47 lives**

December, 2016

Note: *In front of the television on December 15, 2016, I heard that* ***"This might be the last day you will hear my voice and see me"*** *from a 10-year-old Yasmeen Qanouz, one of the dozens of orphaned children who were still trapped in eastern Aleppo. Then another voice,* ***"Please get us out,"*** *pleaded by a little girl, surrounded by almost 50 other children in a heartbreaking video from the city's underground Moumayazoun Orphanage.* ***"We want to live like everyone else."***

This video, recorded by orphanage director Asmar Halabi and released by the Syrian American Medical Society, consistently made me weeping; it portrayed that the children huddled together in winter hats whereas the youngest one was appearing to be a toddler.

Over the past two years, I have been continuously furious at the growing number of tragic imagery in Syria. What a page of war crimes in human history of the 21st century! Where was the Nobel Peace Laureate President Obama at that particular moment? Was he totally occupied with his farewell parties at the White House and even did not have a few minutes to order his staff of the State Department to help these poor children out? Shame, shame, shameeeeeeeeeeeeeeeeeee!!

A REQUIEM FOR NANKING'S 1937 MASSACRE

I Theme

Inches away from the map, may our requiem for 1937 in Nanking
Let da brass, winds and drums orchestrate with marcato G string
Voice for graveless victims of that Rape against Samurais' swords
And thou fallen petals, in soliloquy, echo what temple bell ringing

II Variation

Inches away from **the map,** mappppppppppppp
may our requiem for **1937 in Nanking**
Nankinggg

Let da brass, winds and drums orchestrateeeeeeeeeeeeeeeeee
with **marcato G** string

*Voice for graveless vic*t**ims of that Rape** *against* **Samurais'**
swords
swords,**swords,***swords,****swords,***swords,****swords,***

swordsssssssssssssssssssssss

And thou ***fallen petals,*** *in soliloquy, echo what* ***temple bell*** *ringing*
ringing*inggingingingingingingininingingingingingingingggggggggggggggggggggggggggg*

Note: Marcato is an Italian musical term for stressed bowing to play with forceful dynamic accents over the indicated note(s).

Over a period of six weeks starting on December 13 of 1937, the day that the Imperial Japanese soldiers captured China's then capital Nanking (Its current Romanization is Nanjing), over 300,000 civilian and disarmed combatants were murdered by the Japanese troops; the Japanese soldiers also gang-raped over 20,000 females, including the seniors and minors, and robbed/destroyed countless valuable economic and cultural properties. It was found under the 1947-Tokyo-War-Crimes-Tribunal Court's documents that there had been murdering contests among the Japanese Army officers for killing every 100 people by using the same sword (百人斬り競争 hyakunin-giri kyōsō) during their invasion of China.

Fortunately, fifteen Westerners remained to stay in the City and formed a committee, namely the International Committee for the Nanking Safety Zone, led by German businessman John Rabe (1882-1950), American missionary/educator Wilhelmina "Minnie" Vautrin (1886-1941) and John Magee (1884-1953), in the western quarter of the City that had provided temporary protective shelter and medical assistance for female victims. Together, their combined efforts saved over 20,000 lives.

Japan's war crime on the kidnapping, abduction, torturing, trafficking and gang rape of females, that the victims encompassed females from Asia, Europe and America, had been spreading over various cities in Asia during the World War II. Today for both Chinese/Korean scholars and the general public, it is still painful to recall the atrocities caused by the Imperial Japanese soldiers because that has been a nation's shame. These Asian nations are extremely angry that so far the Japanese Government has still denied the facts of these uncivilized atrocities committed by their Imperial Army.

[INSPIRED BY A CHINESE POEM I COMPOSED IN NANJING ON 12-13-2007]

〈金陵祭〉

天涯咫尺祭金陵　簫管壓弦傾輓情　起板招魂冤不息　落紅離岸覓淒聲

A PATHÉTIQUE CANTATA FOR THE VULNERABLE OF JUNE 4, 1989

A dot/an eternal light, in sight
Across a chronically smoggy sky
Survivors sounded off--in bitter mess
Requiem symphonized for ye unsung victim
Thirty year--**beloved gone--thou body/soul** *torn*
Thug *enthroned by shooting of the one-gang corruption*
Armored tank stopped by an unarmed man's empty hands
Widow day to day licks up two dry lips for not being kissed
Lost-teeth dad's chilling fingers pluck empty bed of his deceased
Over ten thousand nights: heart clock beats tick-tock, tick-tock, sick, kick
Beyond killing field--arrest warrant/detention/torture/imprisonment: fears, tears
Killer ordered thousands of the killed to be burned into ash, his guilty fear down in panic
Chased after by tanks/bayonets, flood of hunger-strike voices yelling to convict Fascism guilty
Blood/flesh splashed amid waves of da fatal dum bullets in front of a Capital's Forbidden City
Tons of camera loyal to justice let facts under your damn censor release for global public
Nightmare: fugitive/fleeing/smuggling/exiling/collapsed for missing many dears
Over ten thousand dead counted, carved at annals: click, quick, click, sick
Silver-haired mom wishes her beloved home for the New Year Feast
Father's hug, the bereft childhood fantasizing for, being ***missed***
By propaganda the picture over years has been banned
Set to envision what billions' dream on democratization
Da June 4 Statue shall lead nation's spirit reborn
Scores not toned for melodies--**nor rhythm**
Stringing bars of legato notes to bless
Zoom in smiling faces **over** *the fly*
Thou voiceless at lonely night

Chased after by tanks/bayonets, flood of hunger-strike voices yelling to convict Fascism guilty
Killer ordered thousands of the killed to be burned into ash, his guilty fear down in panic
Beyond killing field--arrest warrant/detention/torture/imprisonment: fears, tears
Over ten thousand nights: heart clock beats tick-tock, tick-tock, sick, kick
Lost-teeth dad's chilling fingers pluck empty bed of his deceased
Widow day to day licks up two dry lips for not being kissed
Armored tank stopped by an unarmed man's empty hands
Thug *enthroned by shooting of the one-gang corruption*
Thirty years--**beloved gone--thou body/soul** *torn*
Requiem symphonized for ye unsung victim
Survivors sounded off--in a bitter mess
Across a chronically **smoggy sky**
A dot/an eternal light, in sight
Thou ***voiceless*** *at* ***lonely night***
Zoom in smiling faces **over the fly**
Stringing bars of legato notes to bless
Scores not toned for melodies--**nor rhythm**
Da June 4 Statue shall lead nation's spirit reborn
Set to envivion what billions' dream on democratization
By propaganda the picture over years has been banned
Father's hug, the bereft childhood fantasizing for, being ***missed***
Silver-haired mom wishes her beloved home for the New Year Feast
Over ten thousand dead counted, carved at annals: click, quick, click, sick
Nightmare: fugitive/fleeing/smuggling/exiling/collapsed for missing many dears
Tons of camera loyal to justice let facts under your damn censor release for global public
Blood/flesh splashed amid waves of da fatal dum bullets in front of a Capital's Forbidden City

Blood/flesh splashed amid waves of da fatal dum bullets in front of Capital's Forbidden City
Chased after by tanks/bayonets, flood of hunger-strike voices yelling to convict Fascism guilty
Killer ordered thousands of the killed to be burned into ash, his guilty fear down in panic
Tons of camera loyal to justice let facts under thy damn censor release for global public
Nightmare--fugitive/fleeing/smuggling/exiling/collapsed for missing many dears
Beyond killing field--arrest warrant/detention/torture/imprisonment--fears, tears
Over ten thousand nights: heart clock beats tick-tock, tick-tock, sick, kick
Over ten thousand dead counted, carved at annals: click, quick, click, sick
Lost-teeth dad's chilling fingers plucking empty bed of his deceased
Silver-haired mom wishes her beloved home for the New Year Feast
Widow, day after day, licks up two dry lips for not being kissed
Father's hug--the bereft childhood fantasizing for--being missed
Armored tank stopped by an unarmed man's empty hands
Under propaganda that picture over years has been banned
Thug enthroned by shooting of the one-gang corruption
Set to bury in what billions' dream for democratization
Thirty years--beloved gone--thou body/soul torn
Da June 4 Statue shall lead nation's spirit reborn
Requiem symphonized for ye unsung victim
Scores not toned for melodies--nor rhythm
Survivors sounded off--in a bitter mess
Stringing bars of legato notes to bless
Zoom in smiling faces over the fly
Across a chronically smoggy sky
Thy voiceless at lonely night
A dot, *eternal light,* ***in sight***
Voices to **Liberty ignite**
A Song for the Bright

Note: During the months of April and May in 1989, hundreds of thousands of college students, from over forty cities, gathered at the **Tiananmen Square**, outside of the Forbidden City at the Capital City **Beijing**. The students protested against waves of inflation and an organized-corruption network among government officials' families; they appealed for a full scale of democratization.

INSPIRED BY MY CHINESE POEMS

<三十年來魂魄溺>---調寄蝶戀花

紫禁城前瀟雨亟，娃輩書生，餓諫心酸澀。一夕罡風崩社稷，焚屍滅跡春秋識。
月落床前鐘答滴，油盡爹娘，喪子誰憐惜。三十年來魂魄溺，鵑啼泣竭詩腸辟。

<昭昭覓.塚亡靈>---調寄聲聲慢

魂魂激激, 魄魄瀟瀟, 洶洶湧湧汨汨, 陸肆荆歌還憶, 魅魑纏逼。
公車奏諫絶食, 怎詎招佞臣躉斥。 達彈擊, 戮英才, 影像録, 人間悉。
喚女呼兒悽戚, 殤劫恨, 含冤泣聲孤寂。 孽障難逃, 法眼豈容竄匿。
昭昭覓, 鼙鼓響, 塚亡靈。淅淅瀝瀝, 輯史簡, 究板蕩傾筆擲戟。
註: 達彈乃達姆彈

<索微言 . 刻弔言>---調寄鷓鴣天

血肉腥風血禍連, 冷槍霹靂叫崩天, 一呼中彈多蒙難, 慘見橫屍皆少年。
冤未解, 痛蔓延, 斷腸枯眼最堪憐。御坊未奏安魂曲, 求索微言刻弔言。

<殤祭>

血染衙前魘夢纏　無辜罹難正英年　千家喚女呼兒喪　一戶封侯鎖庶言
廿載含冤休輓曲　九州尋路撒溪錢　人間浩氣應猶在　擊鼓魂招司馬遷

<花都哀國是>

花都霧冷道辛酸　圓缺陰晴孰兩全　攬月狂歌哀國是　招魂絶處共嬋娟

<斥登徒折楚>---調寄破陣子

詠嘆騷魂山鬼, 九歌雲水瀟湘, 汨八年英雄血淚, 三捷長沙憑土槍, 芷江浩氣彰。
嘆斥登徒落第, 登基折煞倫常, 折亘古荆風楚雅, 折辱周公拆棟樑, 枉燒萬歲香。

<賦輓忠魂骨>

萬劫天讎萬里歌　狂歌浩浩唱黄河　山河寸寸遺忠骨　賦輓英魂賦奈何

<拍欄憶汨羅>

滾滾驚濤泣輓歌　昭昭浩氣覓蕭何　浪花淘盡英雄夢　拍遍欄杆憶汨羅

<血肉肇狂歌>

萬惡權謀肇劫波　狂沙萬里我狂歌　山河血肉驚山鬼　不懼河殤竊賊多

In expressing their sympathy to the sudden death of the marked-off General Secretary Hu Yaobang of the Chinese Communist Party (in a position equivalent to China's President) in April, who had a reputation for being dignified and liberal, local students gradually turned to a widespread class boycott. For the purpose of drawing international attention, tens of thousands of students began a hunger strike and set up camp-in-occupation at the Square on May 13, two days prior to the state visit of the Soviet Union President Mikhail Gorbachev whereas the students' occupation had continued up to June 4. At the height of the demonstration, over a million students and civilians came up to the Square. Eventually on May 19, the behind-the-curtain senior members of the Communist Party officially denounced the students as reactionary for committing a crime of bourgeois liberalization. Martial law was declared by Premier Li Peng on the next day; meanwhile the dovish General Secretary Zhao Ziyang was removed from office and immediately put under house-arrest, without going through due process, until his death in 2005. According to the most recently declassified information from Western government sources, starting from the early morning on June 4 and continuing for several days, over 250,000 soldiers had been called in to crack down and clear the Square and the City, which resulted in over 10,000 students and civilians being killed under tanks and by automatic rifles.

Dumdum bullets, which have been **prohibited** from use in any war conflicts under the **International Committee of the Red Cross's** customary international law study, are projectiles designed to expand a larger diameter wound for faster incapacitation. During the crack-down on June 4, 1989 in Beijing, local medical personnel were extremely saddened that most of the wounded patients who had been send to the emergency rooms were shot by the dumdum bullets; the physicians found no way to save these precious young lives.

Legato is an Italian musical term that indicates a phrase being played smoothly and connectedly without any perceptible interruption between the notes. An ***eternal light***, eternal flame, or everlasting light is an icon that, under either the Jewish or Christian traditions, refers to a continuous lamp or candle burning in a sin-darkened world. ***Cantata*** is a vocal composition based on a narrative text, in a form consisting of a number of movements, such as arias, recitatives, duets and choruses; however stage design and costumes are not employed.

LIFE

&

POETRY

A SYMPHONIZED VOYAGE
OF
ONE HUNDRED YEARS

Off a fishing port entry
End of da 19th century
Eight-year boy's dad sick death
Boy fed grandmom until she left
Teenaged orphan's dream be sought
At Macau, he dared jumping onto board
Wooden boat sailed for cross-oceanic voyage
Over the storm, for months, to a golden village
For over ten years, working for fifteen hours every day
Never in school, dreamed schooling for his kid that may
Selling ID, back to hometown with dream of fortune/property
Money unexpectedly cheated by learned cousin—yelling/misery
So left behind a two-year son & wife, voyaging 2nd time to Ellis Island
Whom, with no ID, yelled by the Immigration under an arrest warrant
Faceless, speechless, hopeless, a body found on Hudson River, motionless
His son, of da Flying Tigers, at River recalled how dad needed to be tearless
When a voyage voicing through two continents via symphony of hundred years
What da requiem symphonized voices of war/peace, life/death for human dears
Echoing to a home legacy for singing grace to the needed with a generous hospitality
Where three great-grand kids now bowing tunes on thy heart-strings at la Capital City

NOVEMBER 1, 2017

Note: This is a poetic family tree **in memoriam of my grandfather, Tai-Yik Chan** of Zhong Shan County in China's Guangdong Province, who was rejected for his re-entry by the Immigration Services for being unable to provide proof of identification; he died on the Hudson River in 1930.

Grandfather started to work as a fisherman at the age of eight, for earning money to feed his grandmother, at a time when his father died of unknown sickness and mother left the family; he never went to school and at his late teens, got on board of a wooden boat in Macau, which was at time a Portuguese colony located next to Hong Kong in Asia, on a trip for several months, crossing the Ocean to the United States. Upon his arrival in New York, he started to work as a slavery labor for the laundry services for almost fifteen hours each day. Over a period of more than ten years, he estimated he had saved sufficient money for making a beautiful fortune at his hometown; he then sold his identification card and sailed back to Macau. A year later, only after he had married and purchased his first house, he suddenly found out that the largest sum of monies, that he previously sent home to his cousin who was the only learnt and bilingual person from his village, prior to his return to Macau from the United States, had been cheated and was totally gone—The cousin inexcusably declared that all properties and stocks, that had been purchased on behalf of grandfather, were only deeded under the cousin's sole ownership that the cousin refused to transfer these titles/deeds back to grandfather's interest. As a result, grandfather was financially forced to leave his two-year old son and wife behind in Macau the next year, for taking a second voyage, over the stormy waves for months, back to the United States again. With no identification card in hand in front of the U.S. Immigration counter, he was rejected for his entry to Ellis Island for inspection; he stayed in the boat which was moored along the Hudson River for a period of time. Being miserable and hopeless, he collapsed and eventually jumped into the River....

In the spring of 1993, it was the first time I speechlessly accompanied my father, who served for the U.S. Flying Tigers during the Second World War, to walk along the shore of the Hudson River in New York. Tonight speechlessly again, I pray for my grandfather and father, and report to them that my three children now are successful professionals working and residing in the Capital city; they indeed feel grateful for their **family tree rooted across the ocean over a passage of one hundred years.**

A PASTORAL FUGUE SONATA

Exposition of Theme I: A Glimpse of Zen Purity

At the corner of a bamboo pavilion alone
Plucking a lute, singing loud on head tone

Deep inside a wood why cares the tune
For drawing brightened one from moon

Mirroring soundlessly on thy glassy lake
Cloud under skylight clicks/clicks, clicks

Mindset, in a glimpse, clicks to be Zen-pure
For learning the source of a flowing sphere

Exposition of Theme II: In Search For A Short Life Taste

Over snow-blanketed grassland, black motions are the cows
Who have been silently feeding babies for ages, be so proud

Waving storms of cottony flower, snow, snow, snow
Ho, ho, ho, where is that Robin Hood's arrow & bow

Lines of sole driver
Driving along river

Hill behind mountain
Voicing be important

A dreamy image of snow-white
Snow not separated from white

Lingering mind, off thy sight
Two hands on la wheel tight

Ice, frost never bound for a single database
Trip after trip, in search for a short life taste

Development of Theme I: A Glimpse of Zen Purity

At the corner of a bamboo pavilion
alone
Plucking a lute, singing loud on
head tone

Deep inside a wood why cares
that tune
For drawing a brightened one
from moon

Mirroring soundlessly
on thy glassy lake
Cloud under da skylight
for a click, click

Mindset, in a glimpse, clicks to be
Zen-pure
For learning the source of
A flowing sphere

Development of Theme II: In Search For A Short Life Taste

Over snow-blanketed grassland, black motions are the cows
Who have been silently feeding babies for ages, be so proud

Waving storms of cottony flower, snow, snow, snow
Ho, ho, ho, where is that Robin Hood's arrow & bow

Lines of sole driver
Driving along river

Hill
behind
mountain
important
Be
Voicing

A dreamy image of snow-white
Lingering mind, off thy sight

Snow not separated from white
Two hands on la wheel tight

Ice/frost never bound
For a single database

life taste
Trip after trip, in search for a short

Recapitulation of Theme I: A Glimpse of Zen Purity

For learning the source of a flowing sphere

At da corner of bamboo pavilion alone

Drawing bright one from moon

Cloud is in tangling mood

Skylight clicks and clicks

Plucking my lute

Tonguing a flute

Mirroring ye glassy lake

Deep, deep inside a wood

Who hears, who minds that tune

And cares singing loud on head tone

Mindset, in a glimpse, clicks to be Zen-pure

Recapitulation of Theme II: In Search For A Short Life Taste

Who have been silently feeding babies for ages, be so proud

Ho, ho, ho, where is that Robin Hood's arrow & bow

Trip after trip, in search for a short life taste

A dreamy image of snow-white

Two hands on wheel tight

Hill behind mountain

Driving along river

Lines of sole driver

Voicing be important

Lingering mind, off thy sight

Snow not separated from white

Ice, frost never bound for a single database

Waving storms of cottony flower, snow, snow, snow

Over snow-blanketed grassland, black motions are the cows

Note: ***Fugue,*** a kind of technique and art form for music composition that had been matured during the Baroque Period, is written with a contrapuntal texture consisting of a number of individual voices being organized according to certain principles.

Joseph Haydn and Wolfgang Amadeus Mozart, of the Classical Period, are generally praised as the two masters who had pioneered in employing the ***sonata-allegro form*** to compose music with a matured tonal structure--which mostly used for the first movement of a ***sonata and concerto--*** consisting of three sections: Exposition of the thematic subjects, Development, and Recapitulation of the themes. That formal structure can be illustrated by the scheme of: 1) statement, 2) variation/development of the statement for a display of tension, and 3) restatement for relaxation, i.e. A B A'.

The conventional English term ***Zen*** is derived from the Japanese pronunciation of the Chinese word 禪 that **originated from the "*Chan Buddhism*"** 禪宗 **from China** during the fifth century. Its basic practice, de-emphasizing the normativity of any doctrines, is immersed into a mental state through calm and silent **meditation for the purpose of reaching a mindset** of self-awareness in **blending with the *yin-yang* integration of the *Taoistic aesthetics*.**

For a trip of five hours, it had been a precious gift driving by myself from **Roanoke of Virginia** back to Washington under the flurries of snow in December, enabling me to experience the farm culture of the **historic south**, especially on my short visit to a small town, **New Market**.

SNAPPED WITH VIBRATO IS THE WIND IN THE WILLOW

In chilling myth, my dream ***was stolen.***
And the citadel of *a legacy has fallen.*
Snapped with vibrato is The Wind in the *Willow.*
In a fugue, an aria melodizes with one *solo oriole.*
Who'd catch a shooting star amidst the **rainy haze?**
Dragon's loch I repose, flush'd with wine **in a daze.**

Who would poke at the setting moon with a sword?
A stabbing shadow, not a single sound, nor a word.

Away from wenches**, or a gambling mall.**
And dancing with fireflies **in a starlit ball.**
On a Pegasus, hairy troubadour had crossed the ocean to the **West'ing.**
Layin' on a spear, with bushy beard'd, *musketeer took his oar knoc'ing.*

Note: ***Troubadour*** is a class of the 12th and 13th-century poet-musicians, of southern France, who used vernacular languages to compose songs for their vocal performance. In recalling the imagery of ancient China's ***Six Arts***, whereas **a philosopher/poet was also trained to be a swordsman,** I hereby revitalize a passage which was firstly translated by my good friend **Cecil Ho** from a classical Chinese ***ci poem*** that was composed by me in 2015. Compliments on this piece of verse, if there is any, should be credited to Mr. Ho's major penmanship. Heartfelt thanks to Cecil. ***Fugue,*** a kind of art form for music composition that had been matured during the Baroque Period, is written with a contrapuntal texture consisting of a number of individual voices being organized according to a certain principle of imitative counterpoint.

INSPIRED BY MY CHINESE POEM

<風拂柳揉輕>—調寄浪淘沙

風拂柳揉輕, 韻協鶯鳴.
問誰烟雨摘流星, 醉卧龍潭挑落月, 劍影無聲.

疏俗色豪庭, 緊貼流螢.
青絲飲馬過西荆, 虬髯枕戈舟楫擊, 夢冷城傾.

—詠智

REST IN PEACE, MY SISTER

Never imagine a storm would peel off my candlelight
Nor cadence note could move my pen out of thy sight
Tick-tock clock beats, via fugue, with mom's weeping
To a buried flower, farewell aria silent at unsung night

Note: **Buried flower** symbolizes the farewell of a beloved one in traditional Chinese literature.

INSPIRED BY MY CHINESE POEM 〈輓家姊詠詩〉

罡風刮落點燈油　一夜無眠筆未收　更漏滴聲聞母泣　輓詩難遣葬花愁

詠智

A BLESSING MESSAGE

Sister,

Our family dream started from squeezing together in a 250-square-feet-government-housing studio for a household of seven in Hong Kong six decades ago. During our childhood, you passed through series of open and competitive examinations, from elementary, secondary to college-bound matriculation. You did not continue for college study only for the purpose of letting your siblings-- Me, WM and WK, have your financial support that enabled us for going to local and overseas colleges. However you passed through all levels of banking compliance license examinations that officially qualified you, even as a high school graduate, to retire from the executive position of Deputy General Manager from the Hong Kong Tokyo/Mitsubishi Bank, Japan's largest bank.

What made you accomplished in your professional career, during the forty years at the Bank, had nothing been based on any personal connection or temporary luck. Hundreds of your classmates, friends and colleagues came to say farewell at your funeral service. That clearly portrayed an eternal record for what you had contributed in life. Those Indian/ Sri Lankan orphans, to whom you had financially supported for their schooling in the past, could be professionally well established today; they did not come to your funeral service. However, you and I would tone the same note from our heart, "It is fine because that is our family legacy for never requesting ensuing reward/return for extending our hands to the needed."

Life is a unique journey for everybody. Everybody feels proud and missing of you, especially my children YW, YL and YF.

Rest in peace!

A PRAISING GRACE FOR GRACE CAVALIERI

Poet/playwright/educator/host/producer/mother/wife, no limit to line of base

Giving thy hands to warm a diverse spectrum of race/age/strata, case after case

Your voice space/pace
For years, just amazed
O sole mio tone & face
Torna Surriento, chase
Libiamo--classic of taste
Tonight toast for Grace

Your voice on air/motion, dedication/demonstration, sound beyond face to face

Praise for sharing the tasted/amazed--Enriching our passion to let poetry in place

Note: ***O sole mio*** (O My Sun) is a popular Neapolitan song composed by Eduardo di Capua in 1898. Also a Neapolitan song, ***Torna a Surriento*** (Come Back to Sorrento) was composed by Ernesto De Curtis in 1902. ***Libiamo ne' lieti calici*** (Let's Drink from the Joyful Cups) is a duet with chorus from opera ***La traviata*** composed by Giuseppe Verdi in 1853.

INSPIRED BY MY CHINESE POEM

相夫教女尚斯文　提掖詩壇幾代人　千載流觴容一醉　只緣今夜適逢君

詠智

Grace Cavalieri *has presented and recorded over 3,000 poets with her program* ***The Poet & The Poem from the Library of Congress****, which she founded, and still serves as Producer/Host. Many of these poets are emerging minorities or foreign born. In addition, Cavalieri has published 20 books and chapbooks of poetry, plus fiction; she has written 26 produced plays, and texts for 2 produced operas; she writes a monthly poetry feature entitled Exemplars for the Washington Independent Review of Books (2011–present).*

NONE BUT AN APPASSIONATA SERENATA:
AN INHERITANCE FROM A FATHER ON CHRISTMAS EVE

Financial assets just momental

Kindergarten to college, my daughters

Touring from city to city of the green sleeves

Smiling with dream for traveler is a must

Eyecatchy tourist guide pricingly fake

Our past footpath mapping over River Thames, London Bridge

Arc de Triomphe, Great Wall, Victoria Peak, White House, and New York Rockefeller

Tonight spot at Joseph's House of Washington, housing for hospice/homeless center

Our serenata footsteps being heard beat after beat, no pitch

Amid flurries, we bring a shortcake

Greet the lonely a heartfelt Merry Xmas

Heart releasing a mutually unsung note free

The only inheritance left from thy father

Where it is spiritually immortal

Over the past three decades, I took or sent my kids travelling to various cultural spots in Europe, Asia and the United States, including but not limited to London, Paris, Beijing, Shanghai, Hong Kong, Singapore, Bangkok, Jakarta, Chicago, New York, to name a few. On the Christmas Eve of 2017, I took my daughters, bringing a shortcake, to visit the Joseph's House on 1730 Lanier Place NW, Washington, DC 20009, where it states that

"Opened in 1990 in response to the AIDS crisis in Washington, DC, Joseph's House offers a welcoming community and comprehensive nursing and support services to homeless men and women with advanced HIV disease and terminal cancer....We believe in love. We nurture and support for our residents."

Note: ***Appassionata*** means passionate in Italian. It is also the name of one of Beethoven's three great piano sonatas that he started to compose in 1804 and finished in 1805 during his second period of career development as a composer, remarkable for his immense passion of wave-after-wave melodic pulses on lyrical liberation, in struggling for a simple but ideal imagery. Beethoven's hearing was rapidly deteriorating during the time when he composed this work. ***Serenata*** ("serenade" in English) is an Italian term for a genre of 18th-century short vocal music with a calm and lyrical character, usually performing in the evening.

GIVE ME A HUG PLEASE…………………………

I Theme

Sipping a coffee mug

Mindset still on the tones of a music clef

Under waves of foggy rain, wiper suddenly popped off

Unlike a musketeer, against the devil, with sword in his hand

That moment only Beethoven's notes toned over a vast land

Breathless for hundreds of seconds, then moving forth

Just kissed goodbye to goddess of death

Please give me a hug

II Variation

                               m
Sipping a coffee u
                               g

Mindset still on the tones of a music clef

Under waves of foggy rain, wiper suddenly popped offfffffffff

           o
Wiper f
           f

Unlike a musketeer, against the devil, with sword in his hand*ddddd*

That moment only Beethoven's notes toned over a vast landddddddddddddd

          O
          r
forth, t
          h…

Breathless for hundreds of seconds, then moving forth

Just kissed goodbye to goddess of death

Please give me a hug*ggggggggggggggggggggggggggggg*

Ashland of Virginia, January 29, 2018

O
N
C
E..............

I Theme

Once crawling on grandmother's lap, no sense of daily bills

Once looking for New Year Eve, a home's ten-course meal

Once leaving parents for going abroad, to an academic hill

Once da life symbolized of rhyme be sealed, never a waste

Once upon mingling nice masters with cosmos view/a grace

Once under lotus shadow, taste of a mountain dew/amazed

II Variation

b
Once crawling on grandmother's lap, no sense of daily i
l
l
s
Once looking for New Year Eve, a home's ten-course meal

h
Once leaving parents for going abroad, to an academic i
l
l
Once da life symbolized of rhyme be sealed, never a waste

g
Once upon mingling nice masters with cosmos view/a ra
ce
Once under lotus shadow, taste of a mountain dew/ama
zed

INSPIRED BY MY CHINESE POEM

〈京都翹楚匯〉---調寄浣溪沙

一夢兒時住屋邨，一家除夕飯團圓，一辭鄉里趁夷船。
一入京都翹楚匯，一緣適韻涉文淵，一依荷影飲山泉。

註:屋邨乃香港戰後興建之廉租屋/華夷之辯及船堅砲利之道乃百年來士人熱衷議題。

MY BEST TOCCATA HEADING TO HEAR

life sits off a gold mine
high to hit for the best
blade fits to bold mind

yesterday was not fine
thine paid the blessed
pressed me out of wine

nightmare is now gone
born today for express
tested for la bugle horn

dears, we, me, for years
clear, no fear to quest
heading my best to hear

Note: *In composing these four stanzas of symmetrical triplets, which are built on an architecture of being contrapuntally rhyming in echo and sequentially interlocking, I had been inspired by Bach's* ***Toccata Fugue in d Minor*** *played by the German Brass.*

CULTURE

&

POETRY

ODE TO THE CAPITOL: TEA SONATA ECHOED BY A CHOIR OF CICADA

Dedicated to Maryland Poet Laureate Grace Cavalieri & Her Poetry Legion

Touchy mist
Lakeside moon
Thy trovatori's soul
May Statue of da Liberty
Mingling at our Times Square
Notes by Dvořák on Hudson River
Spring tunes up thy curve of Annapolis
Dip a tone lipped by a Mall's choir of cicada
Modulate wanderer's melody to that bi-tonal center
Day to night, la NJ Turnpike landing for transportation
Where could those Baltimorean gulls and herons go to hide
By autumn, piece by piece woven over Virginia hill--frosty leaves
Morning light snaps the Pennsylvania maple, atop my rock cliff
Orchid perfume steams up amid Chesapeake's shadowy tide
Town and country, a land of tracking for immigration
Bronze bell at cadence be archaic paideia defender
Sip a cone in echo with the Capitol's sonata
Mirror fluttering firebugs' phosphorus
Generations of the diverse clever
Human praised for being fair
Supersede multi misery
A learnt spirit holds
Your lotus tune
Kissy breeze

Morning light snaps the Pennsylvania maple, atop my rock cliff
Orchid perfume steams up amid the Chesapeake's shadowy tide
Town and country, vast land of tracking for immigration
At cadence, bronze bell be archaic paideia defender
Sip a cone in echo with ***Capitol's tea sonata***
Mirror fluttering **firebugs' phosphorus**
Generations of **multi-diverse clever**
Human praised for being so fair
Supersede the aging misery
Where learnt spirit holds
On your lotus tune
A kissy breeze
A touchy mist
My lakeside moon
Whoever trovatori's soul
May Statue of da Liberty
Mingling at our Times Square
Notes by Dvořák upon Hudson River
Spring tunes up long curve of Annapolis
Dip a tone lipped by a Mall's choir of cicada
Modulate wanderer's melody to that bi-tonal center
Day to night, long NJ Turnpike landing for transportation
Where could those Baltimorean gulls and herons rush to hide
By autumn, piece by piece woven over Virginia hill—frosty leaves

Morning light snaps the Pennsylvania maple, atop my rock cliff
By autumn/piece by piece woven on Virginia hill/frosty leaves
Where could those Baltimorean gulls, herons go to hide
Orchid perfume steams up Chesapeake's shadowy tide
Day to night, da NJ Turnpike landing for transportation
Town and country, a land of tracking on immigration
Modulate wanderer's melody to la bi-tonal center
At cadence, bronze bell be one paideia defender
Dip a tone lipped by Mall's a cappella cicada
Sip a cone in echo with Capitol's tea sonata
Spring tunes up long curve of Annapolis
Mirror fluttering firebugs' phosphorus
Notes by Dvořák upon **Hudson River**
Multi **generations of diverse** clever
Mingling at mutual **Times Square**
Human praised for being so fair
May iconic ***Statue for*** **Liberty**
Supersede the aging misery
Immigrant's trovatori **soul**
What learnt spirit **holds**
There's lakeside moon
Along your lotus tune
And a touchy mist
My kissing *breeze*

INSPIRED BY MY CHINESE POEM

<蟬韻啖清風>—調寄水調歌頭

霜葉立秋織, 禪旭抹江楓。
忘機鷗鷺誰匿, 疏影暗香茸。
落雁平沙弦剔, 流水高山緣覓, 塵劫夢懸空。
移調犯商徵, 聲煞劍如虹。
荷塘月, 明眸奪, 適蓮蓬。
郁濃芳茁, 入腔蟬韻啖清風。
一嘯騷魂筆絕, 幾度銜枚險脫, 談笑識荊雄。
劍膽青山骨, 笳囀叩蟾宮。
—詠智

註: <鷗鷺忘機>/<平沙落雁>/<高山流水 >乃古琴曲; 犯調乃移/轉調; 煞聲乃終結樂句。

Ode is originally a style of the 16th-century classical Latin verse set to songs, similar to a cantata, addressed to a deity. Remarkably Schiller's ***Ode to Joy*** was used by Beethoven as song text in the final movement of his Ninth Symphony, in voicing an ideal seek of universal brotherhood through joy in 1824.

Grace Cavalieri has been appointed by Maryland Governor Larry Hogan as the Maryland Poet Laureate in 2019. Cavalieri and her "legion" of thousands of poetry fans, over the past four decades, have been connecting with each other through the news media/radio/podcasting/ Facebook channels in Washington. That legion of poets portrays a track of multi-generation and multi-culture of immigration originated from different parts of the world. They have been mingling their diverse footpath all over the East Coast of the United States, from New York/New Jersey to Pennsylvania/ Delaware, and down to the Greater Washington Metropolitan area.

Trovatori is a genre of the 13th-century Italian monophonic folk songs with dance performed by poet-musicians. ***Bitonality*** originally is referred to the simultaneous use of two different keys in different parts of a music composition; the term ***bi-tonal center*** is literary used as a metaphor for treasuring the bilingual/bicultural skills of the new immigrants. ***Cadence*** is a musical term referring to a melodic or harmonic formula that concludes, either momentary or permanent, an ending for a section, or a phrase of a music composition.

Paideia is an ancient Greek term in reference to a well-balanced cultivation of mental and physical skills that is comparable to the Confucianism ***Six Arts:*** rites (禮), music (樂), archery (射), horse riding (御), calligraphy (書), and mathematics (數); it is culturally envisioned on enhancing an ideal education for liberal arts.

China's sixty five pieces of **bronze bell-chime set** was excavated in 1978, namely the ***Bianzhong of Marquis Yi of Zeng*** (of 433 B.C.); it reflects the highest level of ancient bronze technology/cultural arts and a sharp application of music theory on the twelve half tones. Except the biggest round shaped one, each of the 64 pieces of leave-shaped bells can sound two different pitches within an interval of either major or minor third, tone-painting an integrated concept of humanity and the **value of an orderly ritual**.

The National Mall, located near the downtown of the District of Columbia, is usually referred to that vast area of grassland between the United States Capitol and the Lincoln Memorial, posturing like a ***dragon meridian*** of the Capital City in terms of ***feng shui***. The Mall encompasses an intellectually enriched landscape of art galleries/cultural programs under the Smithsonian Institution, and various memorials, sculptures and statues; it is generally believed that there has been receiving over 25 million visitors each year. ***A cappella*** is a musical term for unaccompanied choral music.

Czech composer **Antonín Dvořák** (1841-1904) composed his Symphony No. 9, ***From the New World,*** in 1893, which was commissioned by the New York Philharmonic, during a time he served as the Music Director at the National Conservatory of Music of America in New York, 1892 – 1895. In praising for the grandeur and social excitement of America under this ***melting-pot symphony,*** Dvořák organically weaved with different types of folk melodies that he experienced from such a new world, especially the native American Indian songs and African-American spirituals that he had heard; subsequently the theme from the Second Movement (Largo) was arranged into a spiritual-like song ***Goin' Home*** by Dvořák's pupil **William Arms Fisher**, who wrote the lyrics in 1922. Over the past hundred years, this *New World Symphony* has continuously been praised as the most popular "American orchestral work" at concert halls in the West.

The **Hudson River**, a river in New York State with a length of 315 miles, flows from north to south primarily through eastern New York. It significantly goes southward through the Hudson Valley to the Upper New York Bay between New York City and Jersey City that provides a political boundary between the states of New Jersey and New York at its southern end. Numerous landmarks have been built along the River, including the World Trade Center, George Washington Bridge, Lincoln and Holland Tunnels, and the Ellis and Liberty Islands, reflecting an enriching heritage of the European inhabitants' exploration in the East Coast and their ensuing settlement, colonization, revolution, urbanization, industrialization, socio-economic and cultural development, as well as a fully developed multiple-point transportation system. Along with that region's endless infrastructure construction during the twentieth century, the River had always been a hot topic in regard of its confrontation with ecology principles, environmentalism and natural resources management.

The **Times Square**, stretching from West 42nd to West 47th Streets at the heart of Manhattan in New York City, has been positioned as the icon of a melting pot for the "Big Apple", especially for its annual count-down gathering for the millions on the ***New Year's Eve Ball Drop***, and the ***Macy's Thanksgiving Day*** and other ***historic parades***. As the hub of the **Broadway Theater District**, the Square's entertainment show business and the correlated servicing industries have been constantly providing job opportunities to waves of new immigrants in forming an indispensable economic infrastructure for a diverse socio-cultural spectrum. Being one of the world's busiest pedestrian areas, Times Square is also named as one of the world's most popular tourist attractions, drawing over tens of millions of visitors annually whereas hundreds of thousands of people pass through every day whilst many of them are tourists.

The **New Jersey Turnpike** (NJTP), one of the most heavily traveled highways in the United States, is a toll road in New Jersey with a total length of 122.40 miles; it is the most important section of the Interstate Highway System close to the coastal line of the East Coast, facilitating necessary access to various cities and ports in New Jersey, Delaware, Pennsylvania, and New York. **Annapolis**, located on the Chesapeake Bay at the mouth of the Severn River, is the capital city of Maryland. Being surrounded by river, this small beautiful city is part of the Atlantic Coastal Plain and relatively flat, with the highest point being 50 feet above sea level. Annapolis is also considered as part of the Baltimore–Washington metropolitan area.

Siding with Annapolis, the environmentally-well-protected **Chesapeake Bay** has an extended shoreline of 11,684 miles, extending from Northern Maryland to the District of Columbia and Southern Virginia, with an exceptionally valuable feature on the fishing industry (mainly for crabs and oysters) and ecology. It also postures like a ***dragon meridian*** of the Greater Washington metropolitan area in terms of ***feng shui.***

AN EROICA ARIOSO:
ON THE FREQUENCY OF NIAGARA FALLS

I Theme

S/Pounding panoramic sight by dynamic canons of the Niagara Falls
Recall historic arioso, Eroica, sung by Washington/Jefferson/Lincoln
While diatonic mindset sinks, sinking into a bouncing ball, just small
In a montage, frequency for Einstein, Bruce Lee and Jessye Norman

II Variation

Sounding
POUNNNNN**DINGGGGGGGGGGGG**
Panoramic sight by **dynamic canonsssssssssssssssssss**
of the **Niagara Falls**
Recall historic
Arioso**, Eroicaaaaaaaaaaaaaaaaa,**
Sung by Washington, Jefferson, Lincoln
In a montage, frequency
In **sequenceeeeeeeeeeeeeeeee**
For Einstein, Bruce Lee and Jessye Norman
While **diatonic** *set*
MINDSET *TTTTTTTTTTTT*
Sinks, ***sinking*** *into a bouncing ball*
Small, *just*
small.....

Note: **Niagara Falls** is a collective name for three waterfalls on the border of the United States and Canada. For writers and artists, it has always been an unforgettable, powerful, flowing and inspiring metaphysical scenery. Atop the commercial/industrial value on hydroelectric power, its panoramic views on icing-up water amidst frosty smoke, during the winters, vividly portray a brainstorming and adventurous mindset for literary connotation.

George Washington (1732-1799), one of the Founding Fathers of America's Constitutions and Federal government, was a key leader in winning the American Revolution. **Thomas Jefferson** (1743–1826), another one of the American Founding Fathers, had been praised for being the principal author of the Declaration of Independence and later served as the third president of the United States**. Abraham Lincoln** (1809–1865) served as the 16th President of the United States from 1861 until his death from an assassination in April 1865; Lincoln led the United States through the American Civil War for preserving the Union, abolishing slavery, strengthening the federal governance, and modernizing the nation's socio-economics.

Albert Einstein (1879–1955) was a German-born Jewish theoretical physicist who immigrated to the United States in 1933 and developed the theory of relativity; as a 1921 Nobel Prize laureate in Physics, Einstein discovered the law of the photoelectric effect, a crucial step in the development of quantum theory in modern physics. **Bruce Lee Jun-fan** (1940–1973), generally known as Bruce Lee (李小龍), was born in San Francisco and raised in Hong Kong; Lee was a legendary figure for martial arts films in Hong Kong and America of the twentieth century, who successfully developed his physical strength through an integration of western fitness training, healthy nutrition and traditional Chinese martial arts practice, as well as Chinese philosophical metaphor. **Jessye Mae Norman** (1945-2019) had been considered one of the top best American vocalists for opera and lieder in history; Norman had developed a full-range-thorough-voiced Wagnerian repertoire, on the roles of Sieglinde, Ariadne, Alceste, and Leonore. As an African American artist, Norman had spearheaded to reach the top ceiling of the classical-music mainstream and been inducted into the Georgia Music Hall of Fame, Spingarn Medalis, and been receiving several honorary doctorates and other awards, including the Grammy Lifetime Achievement Award, the National Medal of Arts, and member of the British Royal Academy of Music, etc.

Eroica is an Italian word for heroic that is the programmatic title named by Beethoven for his Third Symphony in E-flat major, indicating that "Heroic Symphony Composed to Celebrate the Memory of a Great Man." ***Arioso*** is a genre of solo vocal composition with a lyrical and expressive character, in a style between that of a recitative and an aria, i.e. more melodic than a recitative but shorter in length than an aria. ***Diatonic music*** is referred to notes of a natural scale, either major or minor, without using any chromatic tones. In physics, the term

frequency means the number of vibrations of sound or electron-magnetic wave per second; it may also be used to describe the repetition of certain types of facts or conditions over a periodic process in a range of time.

RE-KISS THY INVISIBLE TIME RING

I Theme

Teaching job, framed like piece of floating brick, clicking to re-kiss thy invisible time r'ng
Dust drops from la lute I touch, pluck and slide for glissando string, a note a life to learn
Hilly brook inside my heart stringing a Zen fantasy of cloud minuet--rhyming an old burn
And a choir of twinkle star accompanies thy surf kayak, on wings of my bel canto sing'ng

II Variation

Teaching *job*, framed like piece of ***floating brick,*** *clicking to* **re-kiss,**
kisssssssssssssssssssss

Thy invisible time r'ng**gggggggggggggggg**

Dust *drops from la lute I touch, pluck and slide* **for glissannnnnndo** ***string***
A **note** a life to
learn

Hilly brook inside **my heart stringing a Zen** *fantasy of cloud minuet*--rhyming an old....
Burn

And a choir of **twinkle star** *accompanies thy* ***surf kayak,*** on wings of my bel canto
sing'ng
Sing'n*gggggggggggggggggggggggggggggggggg*

INSPIRED BY MY CHINESE POEM

<拂弦倚天邊>

漂浮木鐸惜華年　塵落勾彈拂七弦　雲影溪山如夢令　一舟禪籟倚天邊

詠智

Note: I am extremely moved to receive a warm message via Facebook by **John Wineglass**, a three-time ***Emmy awardee*** on movie music composition, who significantly mentioned my humble hands rendering for his growth from the **Washington, DC Youth Orchestra** to the professional field over a passage of thirty years.

My American dream was materialized in 1985 when I was appointed the Development/ Education Director for the Washington, D.C. Youth Symphony Orchestra on planning a **concert tour to China in 1986**. For this task, 108 staff and students performed and visited Qingdao, Jinan, Beijing, Shanghai, Hong Kong, Taipei, Kaohsiung and Tainan, while most students had never left their hometowns. At first, my American supervisor sought to gain financial support from then-Mayor Marion Barry, but it was in vain. So I lunched with a lady staff member of the Mayor's Office and was tipped to prepare a letter signed by ten students from the Orchestra, addressed to the wife of Mayor Barry. The letter pointed out the fact that the underserved students' financial limitation did not allow them to sell raffle tickets for covering their tour costs. Soon Mayor Barry allocated $50,000 from the Escheat Fund and endorsed an official letter for all corporate businesses in the District of Columbia that had ties with China trade to support these underprivileged kids. With these efforts, we were able to bring a full orchestra of students with a big team of staff and chaperones for a month-long concert tour to China, plus making three hundred thousand dollars surplus for a reserve fund at time. What a triumph!

Immediately after our concert successfully performed in Beijing, **US Ambassador Winston Lord** invited the Orchestra for dinner at his official residence. Dan Sutherland, then Washington Post's Beijing correspondent, asked me why the audience was hysterically screaming at the time when I announced that the Orchestra was going to play ***Beethoven's Symphony No. 5,*** the ***Fate Symphony***. I explained to Sutherland that "During the ***Cultural Revolution of 1966-1976***, the ruling govern- ment ignorantly purged Beethoven and all kinds of Western culture; meanwhile the majority of scholars/literati/artists, who had ties to the West, were barbarically tortured. Now these learned bourgeois are officially liberated from their terrible nightmare of persecution!"

Then I recall **Bryan Young,** an internationally-recognized bassoonist and founder of the critically-acclaimed **Poulenc Trio**, is another proud fan of mine from the Youth Orchestra Program; Bryan invited me to his mansion at the Baltimore Inner Harbor for family banquet on July 4, 2014. Together we watched the made-in-China firework after dinner. Also from the Youth Orchestra, **Judy Dines, Toyin Spellman, Nicole Cherry, Jamal Brown, Marcia McIntyre, Leslie Delaine, Elise Cuffy, Kimberly Johnson, Tiffani Perry, Karona Botts Poindexter, Okorie Johnson, and Sarah Garske**, are all accomplished musicians today.

For stringed instruments, ***glissando*** is a technique for executing rapid sliding movement in illustrating a virtuoso effect. ***Bel canto*** is an Italian musical term originally referring to the highly artistic vocal techniques sung for serious opera; conventionally it is referred to the trained techniques for voice projection on the head tone for high notes and chest tone for low notes respectively. Of the seventy-one students who enrolled in my class of ***Survey on Western Classics at Beijing Capital Normal University*** in the spring of 2018, quite a few of these young people have been continuing to communicate with me for seeking of my advice on their literary exploration.

Being in school, ***nightmares*** *to hear* ***time's up,*** *pens*
downnnnnnnnnnnn
Daydreaming **off the schools**, thy lifelong **study** be
founddddddddddddd

Bless you all!

<風雅成追憶>——調寄蝶戀花

猶記兒時流水筆, 穿插科場, 夜夜殫精畢。
高考屈人規矩失, 眠乾睡濕皮依骨。
容嘆今時臨斅席, 多少英才, 汲汲謀官職。
何以疾書匡黍稷, 斷層風雅成追憶。

NOCTURNE FOR A NOBEL PEACE LAUREATE FAN

Dedicated To 2010 Nobel Peace Laureate Liu Xiaobo, A Dissident Writer Who Had Been Detained Behind Bars For Over Five Thousand Days And Was Mistaken As The Leading Author Of The Awarded Prize. Liu Spoke Out For The Billions But Died During His Medical Parole.

One single pen

But tons of fans

You only posted a Charter

Who mistaken the author

Five thousand days, behind bars
Voices for that billions spread far
Pen, not knife, immortally be the rebel
Life mortally not be seated for a Nobel
With handfuls of intercontinental missiles
Writhe to ban single pen's written visuals

Intercontinental missiles materially in hand
Single pen's visuals/writings writhed to ban
Rebel been labelled with no mortal knife
Nobel seat not available to immortal life
Barred behind for thousands of days
Spread voice to billions with no hate

Charter was posted by who

Author mistaken to be you

Bingo of one

Fan for a ton

7-13-2017

Note: This is a melancholy nocturne written to pay my heartfelt tribute to **Liu Xiaobo** (1955-2017), who was awarded the ***Nobel Peace Prize in 2010*** while being imprisoned, whereas over twenty-five percent of his life time had been detained behind bars. Liu was not allowed to leave from China for receiving the Award and **an empty seat was symbolically reserved for him on the stage** during the Award Ceremony; Liu **eventually died during a medical parole** on July 13, 2017.

What a satirical paradox in history it was, when the Norwegian Nobel Committee decided to award the Nobel Peace Prize for 2010 to Liu Xiaobo, partially for his "authorship" behind the manifesto ***Charter 08***, they announced that Liu "was a leading author behind Charter 08." Actually Liu never claimed himself as the original author of the ***Charter 08,*** but mainly acted as an editor/circulator/promoter for that ***Charter.***

However in his 2009 essay that he presented to the Court during the trial in China, Liu entitled that ***"I Have No Enemies".***

Nocturne is a genre of romantic-character serenade music for piano with a melancholy style, on a texture with expressive melodic lines along a broken-chord accompaniment. Frederick Chopin is the best known composer for this kind of genre.

Bingo is a Scottish children's song that its earliest version was published in 1780. Liu requested to have a children's choir singing at his Nobel award ceremony, even though he was NOT allowed to attend that ceremony.

STRINGING TO A TOP NOVELTY: YEAR OF 2019

I Theme

Space-shuttling back & forth over ocean/mountain/darkness/lightning, clicking to online
A click to my new & thy sealed, the Euro-Asia/Afro-America, cosmos zoomed to be mine
A montage of kissing lotus seeded atop la snowy hill, kiss off da mystery, fist off a misery
That pathos/ethos's stringed harmonics touchy onto a top novelty, sonority of my poetry

II Variation

Space-shuttling back & forth over *ocean/mountain/**darkness/lightning,***

clicking to onlineeeeeeeeeeeeeee

A click to my ***new*** & thy ***sealed***, the *Euro-Asia/Afro-America*, **cosmos** zoomed to be

mineeeeeeeeeeeeeeeee

A montage of ***kissing*** **lotus** *seeded atop la snowy hill*

Kiss *off da* ***mystery***

Fist

off

a *misery*

That *pathos/ethos's* **stringed harmonics** touchy onto a top *novelty*

Sonority of my

poetry

INSPIRED BY MY CHINESE POEM

〈梳透九州還〉

網遊梳透九州還　今古華夷點指間　雲頂採蓮甘勝嘆　惜緣弦拂叩秦關

Note: The ***Space Shuttle*** was a partially reusable spacecraft that had been commissioned and operated by the U.S. **National Aeronautics and Space Administration** (NASA) as part of the Space Shuttle program during the period of 1981-2011. ***Online***, in today's telecommunications and computer technology, implies to all sorts of internet connectivity and communications.

Snow lotus, grown well below freezing point at the top of cliff or mountain that is mostly found in the Xinjiang and Mongolian region of China, has been considered a type of miraculously effective herb. However under the popular modern Chinese novel ***The Legend of the Book and the Sword*** by Luis Cha, this rarely available herb is literarily associated with the kind of beauty who has an exceptional character.

The pair of terms ***pathos*** and ***ethos*** are generally believed to have been originated from the Hellenistic classic, the ***Rhetoric*** by **Aristotle** who identifies three artistic modes of persuasion: ***pathos*** (awaking emotion), ***logos*** and ***ethos***. Ethos is also considered to be the origin of the modern English word ***ethics***. For a detailed discussion on the terminology of pathos and ethos, please refer to: ***The Rise of Music in the Ancient Word*** (1943) by **Curt Sachs**.

Harmonics, hereby referring to the so-called "***artificial harmonics***," is a performance technique for stringed instruments by simultaneously stopping and touching lightly at an exact point on the string, producing a unique sound quality of ***"glassy" tone color***, especially on the high range of notes.

HER POET'S EYES SILENCE SORROW

I Theme

Even chilly drops, icy frost freezing la couple's raincoat
His yin-yang oars speed up waves behind a single boat
By dreams of swirling to moon, snapping shore willow
So her poet's eyes tone a swan on lake, silence sorrow

II Variation

E*ven chilly drops,* ***icy frost*** freezing la
couple's rain-
coat*tt*
***H*is** *yin-yang* oars
speed up
waves be-
hind
a ***single***
boat*tt*
B*y** *dreams of* swirling to ***moon, snapping
shore
willow**owowowowowowow**
***So he*r** poet's eyes **tone**
A swan *on*
la*ke*
*si*lence
sorrow***owowowowowowow***

INSPIRED BY MY CHINESE POEMS

<宿鷺醉詩癡>

霜凝雨露貼蓑衣　攬月沿江拂柳枝　一葉輕舟雙楫擊　心湖宿鷺醉詩癡

<九鐵入沙田>

一枕清霜擁卷眠　情懸九鐵入沙田　林蔭道宴千稀記　范克廉樓留萬言

<關中入破急>

涼颸水滸絮飄蓬　晨旭霞衣不待縫　暮入華燈初上夜　尋他破急入關中

<粵韻康乃馨>

會意嫣紅康乃馨　康馨粵韻更形聲　莫愁塵土芬芳失　誰拾春泥識落英

<秋水展眉頭>

湖心浪静鷗鵝浮　沙淨渚清何所求　白鷺回眸天一角　疾依秋水展眉頭

<夏夢適秋鴻>

堪圓夏夢適秋鴻　風急天衢月冷冲　雨歇雲清滄浪逸　不佯朱雀邀江楓

<出鞘一刀傾>

勾彈柳絮拂揉輕　誰吻流星冷雨馨　不畏迷踪掀閉月　飛身出鞘一刀傾

<春露物語儂>

冬霜綺膩月凝溶　春露嚶鳴物語儂　夏韻星移琴酒醬　秋風撫撥睡蓮蓬

<過指落輕塵>

絲弦過指落輕塵　飄入蓮塘月影芬　滾拂揉吟揉九骨　漁樵問答問伊人

<生死亦從容>

瀝膽披肝擊楫衝　去留生死亦從容　八千烏夜波心蕩　眾裏尋他把酒中

<春夏秋冬北西南東詠> [步高啓<梅花>原韻]

春溪點滴潋琴台　夏雨霖鈴桂樹栽　秋月印潭擎酒卧　冬蟲履雪夢鶯來
北征沿路尋幽竹　西渡橫戈嚼苦苔　南韻吟哦飄嘆詠　東籬那得紫陽開

<伏櫪芳草緣>

九脈飛洪瀉九淵　一簾溪潋一枯泉　星垂柳浪流波月　霧鎖銀河咫尺船
沓沓蹄蹄單騎過　瀟瀟覓覓逐山穿　暮年心壯征塵志　伏櫪天涯芳草緣

About the Author

Wing-Chi Chan 陳詠智, Chair Professor for Western Classics at Capital Normal University in Beijing, is a Washington-based poet cum musician and an arts practitioner for the global communities. Chan's poems have been broadcasted and recorded under ***The Poet & The Poem*** at the US Library of Congress in 2015 and been listed/documented under ***A Splendid Wake-up Blog*** of the Gelman Library at the George Washington University, a Greater Washington area project that documents poets and poetry from 1900 to present; Chan has been sitting on the Committee of the ***A Splendid Wake*** program since 2016.

Over the years, Chan has been serving as presenter/host/producer for many cultural events in Washington, including the ***GLOBAL POETRY CONTEST IN COMMEMORATION OF THE 1937 NANKING MASSACRE, RHYMING FOR THE NANKING MASSACRE VICTIMS*** at the **Arts Club of Washington** in 2017, and ***POETRY EXTRAVANGAZA/UNA POESÍA EN ECO POETRY IN ECHO*** at the **George Washington University** in 2016. A wide range of Chan's poetry has been published, including ***MASS FOR NANKING'S 1937: Synchronizing Musics and Tonal Rhyming onto Poetry***, Washington: The New Academia Publishing, 2016 [Being rated for 5.0 out of 5 stars Groundbreaking Masterpiece by literary critic Char Jones, #2 Reader/#8 Top Reviewer on Goodreads/Achiever of NetGalley's 500 Reviews' highest level of distinction at Amazon]; ***A Duo Concerto For Moon & Noon***, under **2015 *MiPOesias*** of Washington; poems under the ***Federal Poets*** in 2018 & 2019. Chan's Chinese poems and articles have been published under the ***Asian Research Center*** of the **University of Hong Kong**, ***Hong Kong Literature, Hong Kong Economic Journal, Mingpao Monthly, Master-Insight.com, Beijing CCT Press***, and various Chinese media.

Chan has lectured/presented academic papers on music and culture at worldwide higher education institutions: Yale, Columbia, George Washington, American, Kingston Polytechnic University in London, Tenri University in Japan, University of Hong Kong, University of the District of Columbia, US Library of Congress, Capital Normal University in Beijing, to name a few.

During Chan's tenure as Development Director for the Washington, DC Youth Symphony Orchestra, he raised millions of dollars to operate the Orchestra's international tours to Moscow, Leningrad, Kalinin, Seoul, Pusan, Paris, Lyon, Amsterdam, Utrecht, Barcelona, Qingdao, Jinan, Beijing, Shanghai, Hong Kong, Taipei, Kaohsiung and Tainan; his artistic/cultural advisory spectrum has been crossing over the ocean, including serving as consultant for the National Endowment for the Arts, New Jersey and South Carolina Arts Commissions, D.C. Mayor's Office, and China National Symphony; D.C. Commissioner for National & Communities Services; Project Director for Meet The Composer New Residencies Program; Vice President for Washington Symphony Orchestra's Board; commentator for Canada's Fairchild Radio and Voice of America; organizer for Asia Pacific Life Insurance Underwriters Association Conference and Aetna Sales Congress; presenter for Macau's Youth Symphony Orchestra's 2013 Concert Tour to the U.S.; external examiner for Master's thesis at New York University.

In 2007, Chan, as choral conductor, took a team of twelve American vocalists to participate in a Memorial Concert for the 70th Anniversary of Nanking Massacre, which included Thomas Young, one of the three best known American tenors.

Photo Gallery

With Prof. Leo Lee of Harvard, publisher Man Cheuk Fei of Master Insight in 2019

Received by the Mayor of Baguio of the Philippines in 1977

At Maryland Poet Laureate Grace Cavalieri's Inauguration Ceremony with Michelle Chung

Meeting with noted historian Prof. Chien Mu in 1979

With Prof. John Wineglass of Stanford, a three-time Emmy Award winner, in 2017

Celebrating my mom's 90th birthday in 2018

Conducting at Washington Arts Club in 2017

Received by US Congresswoman Grace Meng in 2017, with Jason Ho and Nanking Massacre survivor Xia Li

First visit of the Great Wall in 1978

With New York composer Prof. Chou Wen-chung in 2017

With Mrs. & Dr. James Billington, US Congress Librarian, in 2017

At the US Capitol in 2018

With students of my 2018 class at Beijing Capital Normal University

With Maestro Predrag Vasić of United Nations Symphony Orchestra & poet Lai-Fong Wong

I was honor to lecture on Chinese poetry at Yale, received by by Prof. Kang-I Sun in 2018

Poets & Musicians paid tribute to Nanking Massacre victims at Art Club of Washington

Greeted by Prof. Jao Tsung I, noted sinologist, in 2013

With former NEA Deputy Chairman AB Spellman in 2006

www.ingramcontent.com/pod-product-compliance
Lightning Source LLC
Chambersburg PA
CBHW081329190426
43193CB00044B/2898